CLASSIC
BARBECUE & GRILL

CLASSIC
BARBECUE & GRILL

100 STEP-BY-STEP RECIPES IN OVER 500 PHOTOGRAPHS

CHRISTINE FRANCE

southwater

This edition is published by Southwater, an imprint of Anness Publishing Ltd,
Hermes House, 88–89 Blackfriars Road, London SE1 8HA; tel. 020 7401 2077; fax 020 7633 9499
www.southwaterbooks.com; www.annesspublishing.com

If you like the images in this book and would like to investigate using them for publishing, promotions or advertising,
please visit our website www.practicalpictures.com for more information.

UK agent: The Manning Partnership Ltd;
tel. 01225 478444; fax 01225 478440; sales@manning-partnership.co.uk
UK distributor: Grantham Book Services Ltd;
tel. 01476 541080; fax 01476 541061; orders@gbs.tbs-ltd.co.uk
North American agent/distributor: National Book Network;
tel. 301 459 3366; fax 301 429 5746; www.nbnbooks.com
Australian agent/distributor: Pan Macmillan Australia;
tel. 1300 135 113; fax 1300 135 103; customer.service@macmillan.com.au
New Zealand agent/distributor: David Bateman Ltd;
tel. (09) 415 7664; fax (09) 415 8892

Publisher: Joanna Lorenz
Editor: Sarah Ainley
Copy Editor: Beverley Jollands
Designer: Nigel Partridge
Illustrations: Madeleine David and Lucinda Ganderton
Photographers: William Adams-Lingwood, Steve Baxter, John Freeman, Michelle Garrett,
Amanda Heywood, Michael Michaels and Patrick McLeavey
Recipes: Carla Capalbo, Jacqueline Clark, Carole Clements, Nicola Diggins, Tessa Evelegh,
Joanna Farrow, Christine France, Ruby Le Bois and Katherine Richmond

ETHICAL TRADING POLICY

Because of our ongoing ecological investment programme, you, as our customer, can have the pleasure and reassurance of knowing
that a tree is being cultivated on your behalf to naturally replace the materials used to make the book you are holding.
For further information about this scheme, go to www.annesspublishing.com/trees

Previously published as *The Barbecue Book*

NOTES

For all recipes, quantities are given in both metric and imperial measures and, where appropriate,
measures are also given in standard cups and spoons. Follow one set, but not a mixture,
because they are not interchangeable.
Standard spoon and cup measures are level.
1 tsp = 5ml, 1 tbsp = 15ml, 1 cup = 250ml/8fl oz
Australian standard tablespoons are 20ml. Australian readers should use 3 tsp in place of
1 tbsp for measuring small quantities of gelatine, flour, salt etc.
Medium (US large) eggs are used unless otherwise stated.

Main front cover image shows Lamb Burgers with Redcurrant Chutney – for recipe, see page 50.

PUBLISHER'S NOTE

Although the advice and information in this book are believed to be accurate and true at the time
of going to press, neither the authors nor the publisher can accept any legal responsiblity or
liability for any errors or omissions that may be made nor for any inaccuracies nor for any harm or injury that
comes about from following instructions or advice in this book.

CONTENTS

• • •

INTRODUCTION

———※———

However simple, there's something about the chargrilled flavour of barbecued food that makes it taste extra special. Maybe it owes part of its appeal to the fresh air that sharpens the appetite and makes that tantalizing aroma so totally irresistible.

There's nothing new about cooking over charcoal; in fact, it's a method of cooking that has been used in most civilizations throughout history. The basic method has changed little over the centuries, but many modern barbecues are very sophisticated, making the job easier, cleaner and more controllable. Whether you're cooking over a simple pile of sticks or on a top-of-the-range barbecue, outdoor cooking is fun, easy and inexpensive.

There are disputes over the origin of the word barbecue, but one explanation is that it comes from *barbacoa*, an American-Spanish word used by the Arawak tribe of the Caribbean, as the name for the wooden frame that held their food over an open fire as it cooked. The Arawaks were cannibals, so the food we cook today is rather different from their offerings!

Whatever your tastes, this collection of recipes offers new, unusual ideas for your barbecue as well as some traditional favourites. There's something for every occasion, from family meals to entertaining: spicy, fruity and exotic grills using fish, meat and poultry; easy sauces and marinades to turn basic ingredients into something new and special; and luscious, indulgent desserts. For vegetarians, there's a whole chapter of innovative ideas that everyone will enjoy.

Best of all, not only does a barbecue set the cook free from the kitchen but, for once, everyone else will actually want to help with the cooking.

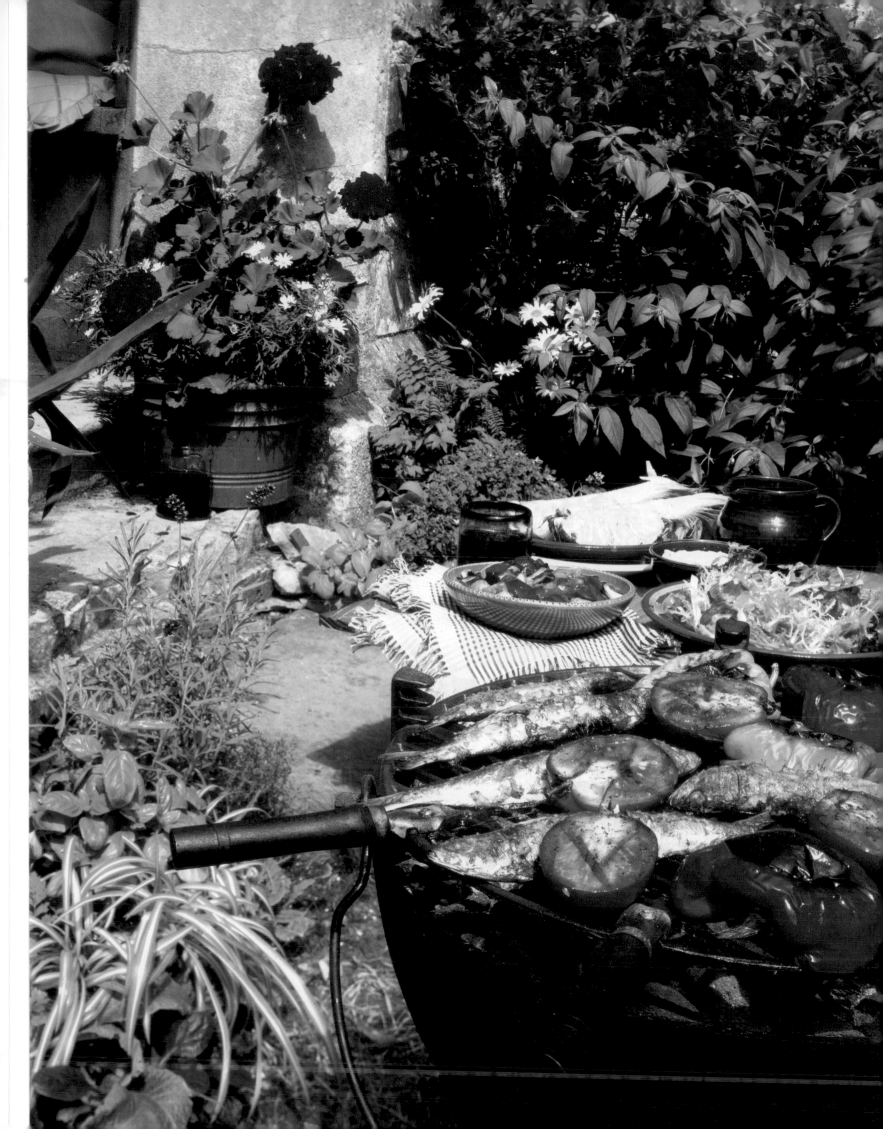

BASIC TIMING GUIDE

· · ·

It is almost impossible to give precise timing guides for barbecue cooking as there are so many factors to consider. The heat will depend on the type and size of barbecue, the type of fuel used, the height of the grill above the fire and, of course, the weather. Cooking times will also be affected by the thickness and type of food, the quality of the meat, and whereabouts on the grill it is placed.

Bearing this in mind, the chart below provides only a rough guide to timing. Food should aways be tested to make sure it is thoroughly cooked. The times given here are total cooking time, allowing for the food to be turned. Most foods need turning only once but smaller items, such as kebabs and sausages, need to be turned more frequently to ensure even cooking. Foods wrapped in foil cook more slowly and will need longer on the barbecue.

TYPE OF FOOD	WEIGHT/ THICKNESS	HEAT	TOTAL COOKING TIME
BEEF			
steaks	2.5cm/1in	hot	rare: 5 minutes
			medium: 8 minutes
			well done: 12 minutes
burgers	2cm/¾ in	hot	6–8 minutes
kebabs	2.5cm/1in	hot	5–8 minutes
joints	1.5kg/3½ lb	spit	2–3 hours
LAMB			
leg steaks	2cm/¾ in	medium	10–15 minutes
chops	2.5cm/1in	medium	10–15 minutes
kebabs	2.5cm/1in	medium	6–15 minutes
butterfly leg	7.5cm/3in	low	rare: 40–45 minutes
			well done: 1 hour
rolled shoulder	1.5kg/3½ lb	spit	1¼–1½ hours
PORK			
chops	2.5cm/1in	medium	15–18 minutes
kebabs	2.5cm/1in	medium	12–15 minutes
spare ribs		medium	30–40 minutes
sausages	thick	medium	8–10 minutes
joints	1.5kg/3½ lb	spit	2–3 hours

TYPE OF FOOD	WEIGHT/ THICKNESS	HEAT	TOTAL COOKING TIME
CHICKEN			
whole	1.5kg/3½ lb	spit	1–1¼ hours
quarters		medium	30–35 minutes
boneless breasts		medium	10–15 minutes
drumsticks		medium	25–30 minutes
kebabs		medium	6–10 minutes
poussin, whole	450g/1lb	spit	25–30 minutes
poussin, spatchcocked	450g/1lb	medium	25–30 minutes
DUCKLING			
whole	2.25kg/5lb	spit	1–1½ hours
half		medium	35–45 minutes
breasts, boneless		medium	15–20 minutes
FISH			
large, whole	2.25–4.5kg/ 5–10lb	low/ medium	allow 10 minutes per 2.5cm/1in thickness
small, whole	500–900g/ 1¼–2lb	hot/ medium	12–20 minutes
sardines		hot/ medium	4–6 minutes
steaks or fillets	2.5cm/1in	medium	6–10 minutes
kebabs	2.5cm/1in	medium	5–8 minutes
large prawns in shell		medium	6–8 minutes
large prawns, shelled		medium	4–6 minutes
scallops/mussels in shell		medium	until open
scallops/mussels, shelled, skewered		medium	5–8 minutes
half lobster		low/ medium	15–20 minutes

MARINATING

· · ·

Marinades are used to add flavour and to moisten or tenderize foods, particularly meat. Marinades can be either savoury or sweet and are as varied as you want to make them: spicy, fruity, fragrant or exotic. Certain classic combinations always work well with certain foods. Usually, it is best to choose oily marinades for dry foods, such as lean meat or white fish, and wine- or vinegar-based marinades for rich foods with a higher fat content. Most marinades don't contain salt, which can draw out the juices from meat. It's better to add salt just before, or after, cooking.

1 Place the food for marinating in a wide, non-metallic dish or bowl, preferably a dish that is large enough to allow the food to lie in a single layer.

2 Mix together the ingredients for the marinade according to the recipe. The marinade can usually be prepared in advance and stored in a jar with a screw-top lid until needed.

3 Pour the marinade over the food and turn the food to coat it evenly.

4 Cover the dish or bowl with clear film and chill in the fridge for anything from 30 minutes up to several hours or overnight, depending on the recipe. Turn the food over occasionally and spoon the marinade over it to ensure it is well coated.

5 Remove the food with a slotted spoon, or lift it out with tongs, and drain off and reserve the marinade. If necessary, allow the food to come to room temperature before cooking.

6 Use the marinade for basting or brushing the food during cooking.

Cook's Tip

The amount of marinade you will need depends on the amount of food. As a rough guide, about 150ml/¼ pint/⅔ cup is enough for about 500g/1¼ lb of food.

BASIC BARBECUE MARINADE

This can be used for meat or fish.

1 garlic clove, crushed
45ml/3 tbsp sunflower or olive oil
45ml/3 tbsp dry sherry
15ml/1 tbsp Worcestershire sauce
15ml/1 tbsp dark soy sauce
freshly ground black pepper

RED WINE MARINADE

This is good with red meats and game.

150ml/¼ pint/⅔ cup dry red wine
15ml/1 tbsp olive oil
15ml/1 tbsp red wine vinegar
2 garlic cloves, crushed
2 dried bay leaves, crumbled
freshly ground black pepper

BELOW: *Marinating foods before cooking adds to the flavour and ensures the food is kept tender and moist.*

STARTERS AND SNACKS

As everyone knows, there is nothing like the aroma of chargrilling food

to whet the appetite. To keep your guests happy while they are waiting

for the main event, begin your barbecue feast with exciting appetizers

that are quick to cook and fun to eat. Here is a collection of

flavoursome and colourful dishes that are guaranteed to disappear

from the grill rack as soon as they're cool enough to snatch away.

There are lots of creative recipes for finger foods to be nibbled with

drinks – from crisp garlic toasts to spicy spare ribs – with plenty of

interesting dips and sauces to dunk them in, as well as delicious

suggestions for elegant starters for more formal meals.

ROASTED GARLIC TOASTS

Barbecuing garlic in its skin produces a soft, aromatic purée with a sweet, nutty flavour.
Spread on crisp toast to make a delicious starter or accompaniment to meat or vegetable dishes.

INGREDIENTS

2 whole garlic heads
extra virgin olive oil
fresh rosemary sprigs
ciabatta loaf or thick baguette
chopped fresh rosemary
salt and freshly ground black
pepper

SERVES 4

1 Slice the tops from the heads of garlic, using a sharp kitchen knife.

2 Brush the garlic heads with extra virgin olive oil and add a few sprigs of fresh rosemary, before wrapping in kitchen foil. Cook the foil parcels on a medium-hot barbecue for about 25–30 minutes, turning occasionally, until the garlic is soft.

3 Slice the bread and brush each slice generously with olive oil. Toast the slices on the barbecue until crisp and golden, turning once.

4 Squeeze the garlic cloves from their skins on to the toasts. Sprinkle with the chopped fresh rosemary and olive oil, and add salt and black pepper to taste.

ROASTED PEPPER ANTIPASTO
· · ·

*Jars of Italian mixed peppers in olive oil are a common sight in supermarkets, yet none can
compete with this freshly made version, perfect as a starter or served with salami and cold meats.*

INGREDIENTS

3 red peppers
2 yellow or orange peppers
2 green peppers
50g/2oz/¹/₂ cup sun-dried tomatoes
in oil, drained
1 garlic clove
30ml/2 tbsp balsamic vinegar
75ml/5 tbsp olive oil
few drops of chilli sauce
4 canned artichoke hearts, drained
and sliced
salt and freshly ground black
pepper
fresh basil leaves, to garnish

SERVES 6

1 Cook the whole peppers on
a medium-hot barbecue, turning
frequently, for about 10–15 minutes
until they begin to char. Cover the
peppers with a clean dish towel and
leave to cool for 5 minutes.

2 Use a sharp kitchen knife to slice
the sun-dried tomatoes into thin strips.
Thinly slice the garlic clove.

3 Beat together the balsamic vinegar,
olive oil and chilli sauce in a small
bowl, then season with a little salt and
freshly ground black pepper.

4 Stalk and slice the peppers. Mix
with the sliced artichokes, sun-dried
tomatoes and garlic. Pour over the
dressing and scatter with basil leaves.

SPICY MEATBALLS

. . .

These meatballs are delicious served piping hot with chilli sauce. Keep the sauce on the
side so that everyone can add as much heat as they like.

2 Add the minced beef, shallots,
garlic, breadcrumbs, beaten egg and
parsley, with plenty of salt and pepper.
Mix well, then use your hands to shape
the mixture into 18 small balls.

3 Brush the meatballs with olive oil
and cook on a medium barbecue, or fry
them in a large pan, for about 10–15
minutes, turning regularly until evenly
browned and cooked through.

INGREDIENTS
115g/4oz fresh spicy sausages
115g/4oz minced beef
2 shallots, finely chopped
2 garlic cloves, finely chopped
75g/3oz/1½ cups fresh white
breadcrumbs
1 egg, beaten
30ml/2 tbsp chopped fresh parsley,
plus extra to garnish
15ml/1 tbsp olive oil
salt and freshly ground black
pepper
Tabasco or other hot chilli sauce,
to serve

SERVES 6

1 Use your hands to remove the
skins from the spicy sausages, placing
the sausagemeat in a mixing bowl and
breaking it up with a fork.

4 Transfer the meatballs to a warm
dish and sprinkle with chopped fresh
parsley. Serve with chilli sauce.

CHORIZO IN OLIVE OIL

*Spanish chorizo sausage has a deliciously pungent taste. Frying chorizo with onions and olive oil
is one of the best ways of using it; you can also cook it on the barbecue, brushed with olive oil.*

INGREDIENTS

*75ml/5 tbsp extra virgin olive oil
350g/12oz chorizo sausage, sliced
1 large onion, thinly sliced
flat leaf parsley, roughly chopped,
to garnish*

SERVES 4

1 Heat the olive oil in a frying pan
and fry the chorizo sausage over a high
heat until beginning to colour. Remove
from the pan with a slotted spoon.

2 Add the onion slices to the pan and
fry until golden. Return the sausage
slices to the pan to heat through for
about 1 minute.

3 Tip the mixture into a shallow
serving dish and scatter with the
roughly chopped flat leaf parsley.
Serve the chorizo on its own or as
a side dish, with warm crusty bread.

Variation

Chorizo is usually available
in large supermarkets and
delicatessens, but any other
similar spicy sausage can be
used as a substitute.

HERB POLENTA

Golden polenta with fresh summer herbs makes an appetizing starter or light snack, served with barbecued tomatoes.

INGREDIENTS

750ml/1¼ pints/3 cups stock or
water
5ml/1 tsp salt
175g/6oz/1 cup polenta
25g/1oz/2 tbsp butter
75ml/5 tbsp mixed chopped fresh
parsley, chives and basil, plus extra
to garnish
olive oil for brushing
4 large plum or beef tomatoes,
halved
salt and freshly ground black
pepper

SERVES 4

3 Remove from the heat and stir in the butter, chopped herbs and pepper.

4 Lightly grease a wide tin or dish and tip the polenta into it, spreading it evenly. Leave until cool and set.

5 Turn out the polenta and cut into squares or stamp out rounds with a large biscuit cutter. Brush with olive oil. Lightly brush the tomatoes with oil and sprinkle with salt and pepper. Cook the tomatoes and polenta on a medium-hot barbecue for about 5 minutes, turning once. Serve garnished with fresh herbs.

1 Prepare the polenta in advance: place the stock or water in a saucepan, with the salt, and bring to the boil. Reduce the heat and stir in the polenta.

2 Stir constantly over a moderate heat for 5 minutes, until the polenta begins to thicken and come away from the sides of the saucepan.

Cook's Tip

Try using fresh basil or fresh chives alone, for a distinctive flavour.

BRIE PARCELS WITH ALMONDS

· · ·

*Creamy French Brie makes a sophisticated starter or light meal, wrapped in
vine leaves and served hot with chunks of crusty bread.*

2 Cut the Brie into four chunks and
place each chunk on a vine leaf.

3 Mix together the chives, ground
almonds, peppercorns and olive oil, and
place a spoonful on top of each piece of
cheese. Sprinkle with flaked almonds.

4 Fold the vine leaves over tightly
to enclose the cheese completely. Brush
the parcels with olive oil and cook on
a hot barbecue for about 3–4 minutes,
until the cheese is hot and melting.
Serve immediately.

INGREDIENTS

*4 large vine leaves, preserved in
brine*
200g/7oz piece Brie cheese
30ml/2 tbsp chopped fresh chives
30ml/2 tbsp ground almonds
*5ml/1 tsp crushed black
peppercorns*
15ml/1 tbsp olive oil
flaked almonds

SERVES 4

1 Rinse the vine leaves thoroughly
under cold running water and dry them
well. Spread the leaves out on a clean
work surface or chopping board.

FIVE-SPICE RIB-STICKERS

· · ·

Choose the meatiest spare ribs you can find, to make these a real success, and remember to keep a supply of paper napkins within easy reach.

2 Mix together all the remaining ingredients, except the spring onions, and pour over the ribs. Toss well to coat evenly. Cover the bowl and leave to marinate in the fridge overnight.

3 Cook the ribs on a medium-hot barbecue, turning frequently, for about 30–40 minutes. Brush occasionally with the remaining marinade.

INGREDIENTS

1kg/2¼lb Chinese-style pork
spare ribs
10ml/2 tsp Chinese five-spice
powder
2 garlic cloves, crushed
15ml/1 tbsp grated fresh
root ginger
2.5ml/½ tsp chilli sauce
60ml/4 tbsp dark soy sauce
45ml/3 tbsp dark muscovado sugar
15ml/1 tbsp sunflower oil
4 spring onions

SERVES 4

1 If the spare ribs are still attached to each other, cut between them to separate them (or you could ask your butcher to do this when you buy them). Place the spare ribs in a large bowl.

4 While the ribs are cooking, finely slice the spring onions. Scatter them over the ribs and serve immediately.

CHICKEN WINGS TERIYAKI STYLE

° ° °

This oriental glaze is very simple to prepare and adds a unique flavour to the meat. The glaze can be used with any cut of chicken or with fish.

INGREDIENTS

1 garlic clove, crushed
45ml/3 tbsp soy sauce
30ml/2 tbsp dry sherry
10ml/2 tsp clear honey
10ml/2 tsp grated fresh root ginger
5ml/1 tsp sesame oil
12 chicken wings
15ml/1 tbsp sesame seeds, toasted

SERVES 4

1 Place the garlic, soy sauce, sherry, honey, grated ginger and sesame oil in a large bowl and beat with a fork, to mix the ingredients together evenly.

2 Add the chicken wings and toss thoroughly, to coat in the marinade. Cover the bowl with clear film and chill for about 30 minutes, or longer.

3 Cook the chicken wings on a fairly hot barbecue for about 20–25 minutes, turning occasionally and basting with the remaining marinade.

4 Sprinkle the chicken wings with sesame seeds. Serve the wings on their own as a starter or side dish, or with a crisp green salad.

TOFU STEAKS

*Vegetarians and meat-eaters alike will enjoy these barbecued tofu steaks. The combination of
ingredients in the marinade gives the steaks a distinctly Japanese flavour.*

INGREDIENTS

1 packet fresh tofu (10 × 8 × 3cm/
4 × 3¼ × 1¼ in), 300g/11oz
drained weight
2 spring onions, thinly sliced,
to garnish
mixed salad leaves, to garnish

FOR THE MARINADE
45ml/3 tbsp sake
30ml/2 tbsp soy sauce
5ml/1 tsp sesame oil
1 garlic clove, crushed
15ml/1 tbsp grated fresh root
ginger
1 spring onion, finely chopped

SERVES 4

1 Wrap the tofu in a clean dish towel
and place it on a chopping board. Put a
large plate on top and leave the tofu for
30 minutes to remove any excess water.

2 Slice the tofu horizontally into
three pieces, then cut the slices into
quarters. Set aside. Mix the ingredients
for the marinade in a large bowl. Add
the tofu to the bowl in a single layer
and allow to marinate for 30 minutes.
Drain the tofu steaks and reserve the
marinade to use for basting.

3 Cook the steaks on the barbecue
for 3 minutes on each side, basting
regularly with the marinade, or fry
them for 3 minutes in a large pan.

4 Arrange three tofu steaks on each
plate. Any remaining marinade can be
heated in a pan and then poured over
the steaks. Sprinkle with the spring
onions and garnish with mixed salad
leaves. Serve immediately.

Cook's Tip
Tofu is easily obtainable
from supermarkets and health
food stores, and is an ideal
alternative to meat.

POLPETTES WITH MOZZARELLA AND TOMATO
. . .

These Italian-style meatballs are made with beef and topped with creamy melted mozzarella and savoury anchovies.

INGREDIENTS
½ slice white bread, crusts removed
45ml/3 tbsp milk
675g/1½ lb minced beef
1 egg, beaten
50g/2oz/⅔ cup dry breadcrumbs
olive oil for brushing
2 beefsteak or other large tomatoes, sliced
15ml/1 tbsp chopped fresh oregano
1 mozzarella cheese, cut into 6 slices
6 drained, canned anchovy fillets, cut in half lengthways
salt and freshly ground black pepper

SERVES 6

1 Put the bread and milk into a small saucepan and heat very gently, until the bread absorbs all the milk. Mash it to a pulp and set aside to cool.

2 Put the minced beef into a bowl with the bread mixture and the egg and season with plenty of salt and freshly ground black pepper. Mix well, then shape the mixture into six patties, using your hands. Sprinkle the breadcrumbs on to a plate and dredge the patties, coating them thoroughly.

3 Brush the polpettes with olive oil and cook them on a hot barbecue for 2–3 minutes on one side, until brown. Turn them over.

4 Without removing the polpettes from the barbecue, lay a slice of tomato on top of each polpette, sprinkle with chopped oregano and season with salt and pepper. Place a mozzarella slice on top and arrange two strips of anchovy in a cross over the cheese.

5 Cook for a further 4–5 minutes until the polpettes are cooked through and the mozzarella has melted.

SKEWERED LAMB WITH RED ONION SALSA

A simple salsa makes a refreshing accompaniment to this summery dish – make sure you use a mild-flavoured red onion that is fresh and crisp, and a tomato that is ripe and full of flavour.

INGREDIENTS
225g/8oz lean lamb, cubed
2.5ml/1/2 tsp ground cumin
5ml/1 tsp ground paprika
15ml/1 tbsp olive oil
salt and freshly ground black pepper

FOR THE SALSA
1 red onion, very thinly sliced
1 large tomato, seeded and chopped
15ml/1 tbsp red wine vinegar
3–4 fresh basil or mint leaves, roughly torn
small mint leaves, to garnish

SERVES 4

1 Place the lamb in a large bowl with the cumin, paprika and olive oil and season with plenty of salt and freshly ground black pepper. Toss well. Cover the bowl with clear film and leave in a cool place for several hours, or in the fridge overnight, so that the lamb fully absorbs the spicy flavours.

2 Spear the lamb cubes on four small skewers. If using wooden skewers, soak them first in cold water for at least 30 minutes to prevent them burning when placed on the barbecue.

3 To make the salsa, put the sliced onion, tomato, red wine vinegar and torn fresh basil or mint leaves in a small bowl and stir together until thoroughly blended. Season to taste with salt and garnish with mint.

4 Cook the skewered lamb on a hot barbecue, or under a hot grill, for about 5–10 minutes, turning the skewers frequently, until the lamb is well browned but still slightly pink in the centre. Serve hot, with the salsa.

CIABATTA WITH MOZZARELLA AND ONIONS

· · ·

Ciabatta bread is readily available and is even more delicious when made with spinach,
sun-dried tomatoes or olives: you can find these variations in most supermarkets.

INGREDIENTS

1 ciabatta loaf
60ml/4 tbsp red pesto
2 small onions
olive oil, for brushing
225g/8oz mozzarella cheese, sliced
8 black olives, halved and stoned

MAKES 4

1 Cut the bread in half horizontally and toast the cut sides lightly on the barbecue. Spread with the red pesto.

2 Peel the onions and cut them horizontally into slices. Brush with oil and cook on a hot barbecue for 4–5 minutes until the edges are caramelized.

3 Arrange the cheese slices on the bread. Add the onion slices and scatter some olives over. Cut in half. Return to the barbecue or grill to melt the cheese.

CROSTINI WITH TOMATO AND ANCHOVY

Crostini are little rounds of bread cut from a baguette and crisply toasted, then covered with a topping such as this savoury mixture of tomato and anchovy.

2 Cut the bread diagonally into 8 slices about 1cm/½in thick and brush with the remaining oil. Toast on the barbecue until golden, turning once.

3 Spoon a little tomato mixture on to each slice of bread. Place an anchovy fillet on each one and dot with the halved olives. Serve the crostini garnished with a sprig of fresh basil.

INGREDIENTS

60ml/4 tbsp olive oil
2 garlic cloves
4 tomatoes, peeled and chopped
15ml/1 tbsp chopped fresh basil
15ml/1 tbsp tomato paste
1 small baguette (large enough to give 8 slices)
8 canned anchovy fillets
12 black olives, halved and stoned
salt and freshly ground black pepper
fresh basil, to garnish

MAKES 8

1 Heat half the olive oil in a frying pan and fry the whole garlic cloves with the chopped tomatoes for about 4 minutes. Stir in the chopped basil, tomato paste and season with plenty of salt and freshly ground black pepper.

Variation

CROSTINI WITH ONION AND OLIVE
Fry 2 large onions, sliced, in 30ml/2 tbsp olive oil until golden. Stir in 8 chopped anchovy fillets, 12 halved, stoned black olives, some seasoning, and 5ml/1 tsp dried thyme. Spread the bread with 15ml/1 tbsp black olive paste and cover with the onion mixture.

MEAT DISHES

———◆———

Succulent grilled cuts of meat are often the starting-point when planning

a meal cooked on the barbecue, and chargrilling gives meat a unique

flavour. A perfect steak or lamb chop, simply seasoned and brushed with

oil before grilling, is utterly delicious. Even ordinary sausages and

burgers for an impromptu family supper can be turned into a treat on

the barbecue. But with a little forethought you can add variety and

originality to your cooking by marinating the meat for a few hours

before you cook it. The simplest marinade will work wonders:

improving the texture and juiciness of the meat as well as adding

the flavours of herbs and spices. The recipes in this chapter draw on

cuisines from all over the world to offer an exciting range of dishes

that are all easy to prepare and delicious.

MIXED GRILL SKEWERS WITH HORSERADISH SAUCE

. . .

This hearty selection of meats, cooked on a skewer and drizzled with horseradish sauce, makes a popular main course. Keep all the pieces of meat about the same thickness so they cook evenly.

INGREDIENTS

4 small lamb noisettes, each about 2.5cm/1in thick
4 lamb's kidneys
4 streaky bacon rashers
8 cherry tomatoes
8 chipolata sausages
12–16 bay leaves
salt and freshly ground black pepper

FOR THE HORSERADISH SAUCE
30ml/2 tbsp horseradish relish
45ml/3 tbsp melted butter

SERVES 4

3 Thread the lamb noissettes, bacon-wrapped kidneys and cherry tomatoes, chipolatas and bay leaves on to four long metal skewers. Set aside while you prepare the sauce.

4 Mix the horseradish relish with the melted butter in a small bowl and stir until thoroughly mixed.

5 Brush a little of the horseradish sauce over the meat and sprinkle with salt and freshly ground black pepper.

6 Cook the skewers on a medium barbecue for 12 minutes, turning occasionally, until the meat is golden brown and thoroughly cooked. Serve hot, drizzled with the remaining sauce.

1 Trim any excess fat from the lamb noisettes with a sharp knife. Halve the kidneys and remove the cores, using kitchen scissors.

2 Cut each bacon rasher in half and wrap around the tomatoes or kidneys.

BACON KOFTA KEBABS AND SALAD

. . .

Kofta kebabs can be made with any type of minced meat, but bacon is very successful,
if you have a food processor.

INGREDIENTS

250g/9oz lean streaky bacon
rashers, roughly chopped
1 small onion, roughly chopped
1 celery stick, roughly chopped
75ml/5 tbsp fresh wholemeal
breadcrumbs
45ml/3 tbsp chopped fresh thyme
30ml/2 tbsp Worcestershire sauce
1 egg, beaten
salt and freshly ground black
pepper
olive oil, for brushing

FOR THE SALAD

115g/4oz/3/4 cup bulgur wheat
60ml/4 tbsp toasted sunflower
seeds
15ml/1 tbsp olive oil
salt and freshly ground black
pepper
handful celery leaves, chopped

SERVES 4

1 Place the bacon, onion, celery and breadcrumbs in a food processor and process until chopped. Add the thyme, Worcestershire sauce and seasoning. Bind to a firm mixture with the egg.

2 Divide the mixture into eight equal portions and use your hands to shape them around eight bamboo skewers.

3 For the salad, place the bulgur wheat in a bowl and pour over boiling water to cover. Leave to stand for 30 minutes, until the grains are tender.

4 Drain well, then stir in the sunflower seeds, olive oil, salt and pepper. Stir in the celery leaves.

5 Cook the kofta skewers over a medium-hot barbecue for 8–10 minutes, turning occasionally, until golden brown. Serve with the salad.

HAM PIZZETTAS WITH MELTED BRIE AND MANGO
· · ·

These individual little pizzas are topped with an unusual but very successful combination of smoked ham, Brie and juicy chunks of fresh mango.

INGREDIENTS

225g/8oz/2 cups strong white flour
10g/¼ oz sachet easy-blend dried yeast
150ml/¼ pint/⅔ cup warm water
60ml/4 tbsp olive oil

FOR THE TOPPING
1 ripe mango
150g/5oz smoked ham, sliced wafer-thin
150g/5oz Brie cheese, diced
12 yellow cherry tomatoes, halved
salt and freshly ground black pepper

SERVES 6

2 Turn the dough out on to a floured surface and knead it for about 5 minutes, or until smooth.

3 Return the dough to the bowl and cover it with a damp cloth or oiled clear film. Leave the dough to prove in a warm place for about 30 minutes or until the dough is doubled in size and springy to the touch.

4 Divide the dough into six and roll each piece into a ball. Flatten out with your hand and use your knuckles to press each piece of dough to a round of about 15cm/6in diameter, with a raised lip around the edge.

5 Halve, stone and peel the mango and cut it into small dice. Arrange with the ham on top of the pizzettas. Top with cheese and tomatoes and sprinkle with salt and ground black pepper.

1 In a large bowl, stir together the flour and yeast, with a pinch of salt. Make a well in the centre and stir in the water and 45ml/3 tbsp of the olive oil. Stir until thoroughly mixed.

Cook's Tip

It's important to flatten out the dough rounds quite thinly and to cook them fairly slowly, or they will not cook evenly. To save time, you could use a 300g/11oz packet of pizza dough mix.

6 Drizzle the remaining oil over the pizzettas. Place them on a medium-hot barbecue and cook for 8 minutes, until golden brown and crisp underneath.

PORK AND PINEAPPLE SATAY

∘ ∘ ∘

This variation on the classic satay has added pineapple, but keeps the traditional coconut and peanut sauce.

INGREDIENTS

500g/1¼ lb pork fillet
1 small onion, chopped
1 garlic clove, chopped
60ml/4 tbsp soy sauce
finely grated rind of ½ lemon
5ml/1 tsp ground cumin
5ml/1 tsp ground coriander
5ml/1 tsp ground turmeric
5ml/1 tsp dark muscovado sugar
225g/8oz can pineapple chunks, or
1 small fresh pineapple, peeled and
diced
salt and freshly ground black
pepper

FOR THE SATAY SAUCE
175ml/6fl oz/¾ cup coconut milk
115g/4oz/6 tbsp crunchy peanut
butter
1 garlic clove, crushed
10ml/2 tsp soy sauce
5ml/1 tsp dark muscovado sugar

SERVES 4

2 Place the onion, garlic, soy sauce, lemon rind, spices and sugar in a blender or food processor. Add two pieces of pineapple and process until the mixture is almost smooth.

3 Add the paste to the pork, tossing well to coat evenly. Thread the pieces of pork on to bamboo skewers, with the remaining pineapple pieces.

4 To make the sauce, pour the coconut milk into a small saucepan and stir in the peanut butter. Stir in the remaining sauce ingredients and heat gently over the barbecue, stirring until smooth and hot. Cover and keep warm on the edge of the barbecue.

5 Cook the pork and pineapple skewers on a medium-hot barbecue for 10–12 minutes, turning occasionally, until golden brown and thoroughly cooked. Serve with the satay sauce.

1 Using a sharp kitchen knife, trim any fat from the pork fillet and cut it in 2.5cm/1in cubes. Place the meat in a large mixing bowl and set aside.

Cook's Tip

If you cannot buy coconut milk, use creamed coconut in a block. Dissolve a 50g/2oz piece in 150ml/¼ pint/⅔ cup boiling water and use as above.

STILTON BURGERS

A variation on the traditional burger, this tasty recipe contains a delicious surprise:
a creamy filling of lightly melted Stilton cheese.

INGREDIENTS

450g/1lb/4 cups minced beef
1 onion, chopped
1 celery stick, chopped
5ml/1 tsp dried mixed herbs
5ml/1 tsp prepared mustard
50g/2oz/1/2 cup crumbled Stilton cheese
4 burger buns
salt and freshly ground black pepper

SERVES 4

1 Mix the minced beef with the chopped onion, celery, mixed herbs and mustard. Season well with salt and pepper, and bring together with your hands to form a firm mixture.

2 Divide the mixture into eight equal portions. Shape four portions into rounds and flatten each one slightly. Place a little of the crumbled cheese in the centre of each round.

3 Shape and flatten the remaining four portions and place on top. Use your hands to mould the rounds together, encasing the crumbled cheese, and shaping them into four burgers.

4 Cook on a medium barbecue for about 10 minutes or until cooked through, turning once. Split the burger buns and place a burger inside each. Serve with salad and mustard pickle.

VEGETABLE-STUFFED BEEF ROLLS

. . .

These Japanese-style beef rolls are very popular for al fresco meals. You could roll up many other vegetables in the sliced beef. Pork is also very good cooked this way.

INGREDIENTS

50g/2oz carrot
50g/2oz green pepper, seeded
bunch of spring onions
400g/14oz beef topside,
thinly sliced
plain flour, for dusting
15ml/1 tbsp olive oil
fresh parsley sprigs, to garnish

FOR THE SAUCE
30ml/2 tbsp sugar
45ml/3 tbsp soy sauce
45ml/3 tbsp mirin

SERVES 4

1 Use a sharp knife to shred the carrot and green pepper into 4–5cm/1½–2in lengths. Wash and peel the outer skins from the spring onions, then halve them lengthways. Shred the spring onions diagonally into 4–5cm/1½–2in lengths.

2 The beef slices should be no more than 2mm/$\frac{1}{12}$in thick, and about 15cm/6in square. Lay a slice of beef on a chopping board and top with strips of the carrot, green pepper and spring onion. Roll up quite tightly and dust lightly with flour. Repeat with the remaining beef and vegetables.

3 Secure the beef rolls with cocktail sticks, soaked in water to prevent them from burning, and cook on a medium barbecue or in a pan over a medium heat, for 10–15 minutes, turning frequently, until golden brown and thoroughly cooked.

4 Blend the ingredients for the sauce in a small pan and cook to dissolve the sugar and form a glaze. Halve the cooked rolls, cutting at a slant, and stand them on a plate with the sloping cut ends facing upwards. Dress with the sauce and garnish with fresh parsley.

VEAL CHOPS WITH BASIL BUTTER

*Veal chops from the loin are an expensive cut and are best cooked quickly and simply.
The flavour of basil goes well with veal, but other herbs can be used instead if you prefer.*

INGREDIENTS

*25g/1oz/2 tbsp butter, softened
15ml/1 tbsp Dijon mustard
15ml/1 tbsp chopped fresh basil
olive oil, for brushing
2 veal loin chops, 2.5cm/1in thick,
about 225g/8oz each
salt and freshly ground black
pepper
fresh basil sprigs, to garnish*

SERVES 2

1 To make the basil butter, cream the softened butter with the Dijon mustard and chopped fresh basil in a large mixing bowl, then season with plenty of freshly ground black pepper.

2 Brush both sides of each chop with olive oil and season with a little salt.

3 Cook the chops on a hot barbecue for 7–10 minutes, basting with oil and turning once, until done to your liking. (Medium-rare meat will still be slightly soft when pressed, medium meat will be springy and well-done firm.) Top each chop with half the basil butter and serve at once, garnished with basil.

SKEWERED LAMB WITH CORIANDER YOGURT

· · ·

These Turkish kebabs are traditionally made with lamb, but lean beef or pork work equally well.
You can alternate pieces of pepper, lemon or onions with the meat for extra flavour and colour.

INGREDIENTS

900g/2lb lean boneless lamb
1 large onion, grated
3 bay leaves
5 thyme or rosemary sprigs
grated rind and juice of 1 lemon
2.5ml/¹/2 tsp caster sugar
75ml/3fl oz/¹/3 cup olive oil
salt and freshly ground black
pepper
sprigs of fresh rosemary, to garnish
barbecued lemon wedges, to serve

FOR THE CORIANDER YOGURT
150ml/¹/4 pint/²/3 cup thick natural
yogurt
15ml/1 tbsp chopped fresh mint
15ml/1 tbsp chopped fresh
coriander
10ml/2 tsp grated onion

SERVES 4

1 To make the coriander yogurt, mix together the natural yogurt, chopped fresh mint, chopped fresh coriander and grated onion. Transfer the yogurt to a serving bowl.

2 To make the kebabs, cut the lamb into 2.5cm/1in cubes and put in a bowl. Mix together the onion, herbs, lemon rind and juice, sugar and oil, then season to taste.

3 Pour the marinade over the meat in the bowl and stir to ensure the meat is thoroughly covered. Cover with clear film and leave to marinate in the fridge for several hours or overnight.

4 Drain the meat and thread on to metal skewers. Cook on a hot barbecue for about 10 minutes. Garnish with rosemary and barbecued lemon wedges and serve with the coriander yogurt.

LAMB BURGERS WITH REDCURRANT CHUTNEY

° ° °

These rather special burgers take a little extra time to prepare but are well worth it.
The redcurrant chutney is the perfect complement to the minty lamb taste.

INGREDIENTS

500g/1¼ lb minced lean lamb
1 small onion, finely chopped
30ml/2 tbsp finely chopped
fresh mint
30ml/2 tbsp finely chopped
fresh parsley
115g/4oz mozzarella cheese
30ml/2 tbsp oil, for basting
salt and freshly ground black
pepper

FOR THE REDCURRANT CHUTNEY
115g/4oz/1½ cups fresh or frozen
redcurrants
10ml/2 tsp clear honey
5ml/1 tsp balsamic vinegar
30ml/2 tbsp finely chopped mint

SERVES 4

1 In a large bowl, mix together the minced lamb, chopped onion, mint and parsley until evenly combined. Season well with plenty of salt and freshly ground black pepper.

Cook's Tip

If time is short, or if fresh redcurrants are not available, serve the burgers with ready-made redcurrant sauce.

2 Roughly divide the meat mixture into eight equal pieces and use your hands to press each of the pieces into flat rounds.

3 Cut the mozzarella cheese into four chunks. Place one chunk of cheese on half the lamb rounds. Top each with another round of meat mixture.

4 Press each of the two rounds of meat together firmly, making four flattish burger shapes. Use your fingers to blend the edges and seal in the cheese completely.

5 Place all the ingredients for the chutney in a bowl and mash them together with a fork. Season well with salt and freshly ground black pepper.

6 Brush the lamb burgers with olive oil and cook them over a moderately hot barbecue for about 15 minutes, turning once, until golden brown. Serve with the redcurrant chutney.

BARBECUED LAMB WITH POTATO SLICES

· · ·

A traditional mixture of fresh herbs adds a summery flavour to this simple lamb dish.
A leg of lamb is easier to cook evenly on the barbecue if it's boned out, or "butterflied" first.

INGREDIENTS

1 leg of lamb, about 1.75kg/4½ lb
1 garlic clove, thinly sliced
handful of fresh flat-leaf parsley
handful of fresh sage
handful of fresh rosemary
handful of fresh thyme
90ml/6 tbsp dry sherry
60ml/4 tbsp walnut oil
500g/1¼ lb medium-size potatoes
salt and freshly ground
black pepper

SERVES 4

2 Use a sharp kitchen knife to scrape away the meat from the bone on both sides, until the bone is completely exposed. Carefully remove the bone and cut away any sinews and excess fat from the meat.

4 Place the meat in a bowl and pour over the sherry and walnut oil. Chop half the remaining herbs and scatter over the meat. Cover the bowl with a clean dish towel and leave to marinate in the fridge for 30 minutes.

1 Place the lamb on a board, smooth side downwards, so that you can see where the bone lies. Using a sharp heavy knife, make a long cut through the flesh down to the bone.

3 Cut through the thickest part of the meat so that you can open it out as flat as possible. Make several cuts in the lamb with a sharp kitchen knife, and push slivers of garlic and sprigs of fresh herbs into the cuts.

5 Remove the lamb from the marinade and season. Cook on a medium-hot barbecue for 30–35 minutes, turning occasionally and basting with the reserved marinade.

Cook's Tip

If you have a spit-roasting attachment, the lamb can be rolled and tied with herbs inside, and spit roasted for 1–1½ hours. A spit makes it much easier to cook larger pieces of lamb.

6 Scrub the potatoes, then cut them in thick slices. Brush with the marinade and place around the lamb. Cook for about 15 minutes, until golden brown.

JUNIPER-SPICED VENISON CHOPS

*Depending on the type of venison available, the chops will vary in size,
so you will need either one or two per person.*

INGREDIENTS

4–8 venison chops
250ml/8 fl oz/1 cup red wine
2 medium red onions
6 juniper berries, crushed
1 cinnamon stick, crumbled
1 dried bay leaf, crumbled
thinly pared strip of orange rind
olive oil, for brushing
salt and freshly ground black
pepper

SERVES 4

2 Add the juniper berries, cinnamon, bay leaf and orange rind. Toss well to coat evenly and then cover the bowl and leave to marinate for at least an hour, or overnight in the fridge.

1 Place the venison chops in a large mixing bowl and pour over the red wine. Using a sharp knife, cut the red onions in half crossways and add them to the bowl.

3 Drain the venison and onions and reserve the marinade. Brush the venison and onions generously with the olive oil and sprinkle with plenty of salt and freshly ground black pepper.

4 Cook the venison and onions on a medium-hot barbecue for about 8–10 minutes on each side, turning once and basting regularly with the marinade. The venison should still be slightly pink inside even when fully cooked.

Cook's Tip

*Tender farmed venison
is now widely available from
supermarkets and good butchers
shops, but if venison is difficult
to find, beef steaks could be
used instead.*

POULTRY AND GAME

Chicken cooked on a barbecue is unfailingly popular with both adults and children, and it can be as simple or sophisticated as you choose: it is very versatile and takes on a whole range of flavours with great success. Buy breast fillets to make delicious kebabs and salads with a minimum of preparation, or cook drumsticks and thighs with robust spicy coatings. Whole birds can be roasted very effectively on a spit, or they can be flattened out by removing the backbone and cooked on the grill rack. It is vital to make sure chicken is always very thoroughly cooked – it needs a medium heat to cook it through without charring the outside. Don't forget other types of poultry, particularly duck, which stays beautifully juicy and moist when cooked on a barbecue.

CHICKEN WITH PINEAPPLE

• • •

The pineapple juice in this Indian recipe is used to tenderize the meat, but it also gives the chicken a deliciously tangy sweetness.

INGREDIENTS

225g/8oz can pineapple chunks
in juice
5ml/1 tsp ground cumin
5ml/1 tsp ground coriander
1 garlic clove, crushed
5ml/1 tsp chilli powder
5ml/1 tsp salt
30ml/2 tbsp natural low-fat yogurt
15ml/1 tbsp chopped fresh
coriander
few drops orange food colouring
(optional)
275g/10oz/2 cups chicken breast
and thigh meat, skinned and boned
½ red pepper
½ yellow or green pepper
1 large onion
6 cherry tomatoes
15ml/1 tbsp vegetable oil

SERVES 6

1 Drain the canned pineapple into a bowl. Reserve twelve large chunks of pineapple. Squeeze the juice from the remaining chunks into the bowl, then discard the chunks. You should be left with about 120ml/4fl oz/½ cup pineapple juice.

2 In a large bowl, blend together the cumin, ground coriander, garlic, chilli powder, salt, yogurt, fresh coriander and food colouring, if using. Pour in the pineapple juice and mix together.

3 Cut the chicken into cubes, add to the yogurt and spice mixture and leave to marinate for about 1–1½ hours. Cut the peppers and onion into chunks.

4 Arrange the chicken pieces, vegetables and reserved pineapple chunks alternately on 6 skewers.

5 Brush the kebabs with oil and cook on a medium barbecue for about 10 minutes, turning regularly and basting the chicken pieces regularly with the marinade, until cooked through. Serve with salad or plain boiled rice.

CITRUS KEBABS

° ° °

Serve these succulent barbecued chicken kebabs on a bed of lettuce leaves, garnished with sprigs of fresh mint and orange and lemon slices.

INGREDIENTS

4 chicken breasts, skinned and boned
fresh mint sprigs, to garnish
orange, lemon or lime slices, to garnish

FOR THE MARINADE
finely grated rind and juice of
1/2 orange
finely grated rind and juice of
1/2 lemon or lime
30ml/2 tbsp olive oil
30ml/2 tbsp clear honey
30ml/2 tbsp chopped fresh mint
1.5ml/1/4 tsp ground cumin
salt and freshly ground black pepper

SERVES 4

1 Use a heavy knife to cut the chicken into 2.5cm/1in cubes.

2 Mix the marinade ingredients together in a large mixing bowl, add the chicken and cover with clear film. Leave to marinate for at least 2 hours, or overnight in the fridge.

3 Thread the chicken on to metal skewers and cook on a medium barbecue for 10 minutes, basting with the marinade and turning frequently. Garnish with mint and citrus slices.

SWEET AND SOUR KEBABS
○ ○ ○

*This marinade contains sugar and will burn very easily, so cook the kebabs slowly
and turn them often. Serve these kebabs with Harlequin Rice.*

INGREDIENTS
2 chicken breasts, skinned and
boned
8 pickling onions or 2 medium
onions
4 rindless streaky bacon rashers
3 firm bananas
1 red pepper, diced

FOR THE MARINADE
30ml/2 tbsp soft brown sugar
15ml/1 tbsp Worcestershire sauce
30ml/2 tbsp lemon juice
salt and freshly ground black
pepper

FOR THE HARLEQUIN RICE
30ml/2 tbsp olive oil
1 small red pepper, diced
225g/8oz/generous 1 cup cooked
rice
115g/4oz/1 cup cooked peas

SERVES 4

1 Mix together the marinade
ingredients. Cut each chicken breast
into four pieces, add to the marinade,
cover and leave for at least 4 hours,
or preferably overnight in the fridge.

2 Peel the pickling onions, blanch
them in boiling water for 5 minutes
and drain. If using medium onions,
quarter them after blanching.

3 Cut each rasher of bacon in half
with a sharp knife. Peel the bananas
and cut each one into three pieces.
Wrap half a bacon rasher around each
of the banana pieces.

4 Thread the bacon and bananas
on to metal skewers with the chicken
pieces, onions and pepper pieces. Brush
generously with the marinade.

5 Cook on a low barbecue for about
15 minutes, turning and basting
frequently with the marinade.

6 Meanwhile, heat the oil in a
frying pan and stir-fry the diced pepper
briefly. Add the rice and peas and stir
until heated through. Serve the
Harlequin Rice with the kebabs.

BLACKENED CAJUN CHICKEN AND CORN

○ ○ ○

This is a classic American Deep-South method of cooking in a spiced coating, which can be used for poultry, meat or fish. The coating should begin to char and blacken slightly at the edges.

INGREDIENTS

*8 chicken joints (drumsticks,
thighs or wings)
2 whole corn cobs
10ml/2 tsp garlic salt
10ml/2 tsp ground black pepper
7.5ml/1½ tsp ground cumin
7.5ml/1½ tsp paprika
5ml/1 tsp cayenne pepper
45ml/3 tbsp melted butter
chopped parsley, to garnish*

SERVES 4

1 Trim any excess fat from the chicken, but leave the skin in place. Slash the thickest parts with a knife, to allow the flavours to penetrate the meat as much as possible.

2 Pull the husks and silks off the corn cobs, then rinse them under cold running water and pat them dry with kitchen paper. Cut the cobs into thick slices, using a heavy kitchen knife.

3 Mix together all the spices. Brush the chicken and corn with the melted butter and sprinkle the spices over them. Toss well to coat evenly.

4 Cook the chicken pieces on a medium-hot barbecue for about 25 minutes, turning occasionally. Add the corn after 15 minutes, and grill, turning often, until golden brown. Serve garnished with chopped parsley.

CHICKEN WITH HERB AND RICOTTA STUFFING
. . .

These little chicken drumsticks are full of flavour and the stuffing and bacon help to keep them moist and tender.

INGREDIENTS

60ml/4 tbsp ricotta cheese
1 garlic clove, crushed
45ml/3 tbsp mixed chopped fresh herbs, such as chives, flat-leaf parsley and mint
30ml/2 tbsp fresh brown breadcrumbs
8 chicken drumsticks
8 smoked streaky bacon rashers
5ml/1 tsp whole-grain mustard
15ml/1 tbsp sunflower oil
salt and freshly ground black pepper

SERVES 4

1 Mix together the ricotta, garlic, herbs and breadcrumbs. Season well with plenty of salt and pepper.

2 Carefully loosen the skin from each drumstick and spoon a little of the herb stuffing under each, smoothing the skin back over firmly.

3 Wrap a bacon rasher tightly around the wide end of each drumstick, to hold the skin in place over the stuffing during the cooking time.

4 Mix together the mustard and oil and brush them over the chicken. Cook on a medium-hot barbecue for about 25 minutes, turning occasionally.

BABY CHICKENS WITH LIME AND CHILLI

o o o

*Poussins are small birds which are ideal for one to two portions. The best way to prepare them
is spatchcocked – flattened out – to ensure more even cooking.*

INGREDIENTS

*4 poussins or Cornish hens, about
450g/1lb each
45ml/3 tbsp butter
30ml/2 tbsp sun-dried tomato
paste
finely grated rind of 1 lime
10ml/2 tsp chilli sauce
juice of ½ lime
lime wedges, to serve
fresh flat leaf parsley sprigs,
to garnish*

SERVES 4

1 Place each poussin on a chopping
board, breast-side upwards, and press
down firmly with your hand, to break
the breastbone.

2 Turn the poussin over and, with
poultry shears or strong kitchen
scissors, cut down either side of the
backbone. Remove it and discard.

3 Turn the poussin breast-side up
and flatten it gently. Lift the breast skin
carefully and gently ease your fingertips
underneath, to loosen it from the flesh.

4 Mix together the butter, sun-dried
tomato paste, lime rind and chilli sauce
in a small bowl. Spread about three-
quarters of the mixture under the skin
of the poussins, smoothing it evenly
over the surface of the flesh.

5 To hold the poussins flat during
cooking, thread two bamboo skewers
through each bird, crossing at the
centre. Each skewer should pass
through a drumstick and then out
through a wing on the other side.

6 Mix the reserved paste with the
lime juice and brush it over the skin
of the poussins. Cook on a medium-
hot barbecue, turning occasionally,
for 25–30 minutes, or until there is
no trace of pink in the juices when
the flesh is pierced. Garnish with lime
wedges and fresh flat leaf parsley.

CHICKEN SALAD WITH CORIANDER DRESSING

Serve this salad warm to make the most of the wonderful flavour of barbecued chicken basted with a marinade of coriander, sesame and mustard.

INGREDIENTS

4 medium chicken breasts, skinned
and boned
225g/8oz mangetout
2 heads decorative lettuce such as
lollo rosso or feuille de chêne
3 carrots, cut into matchsticks
175g/6oz button mushrooms,
sliced
6 bacon rashers, fried and chopped

FOR THE CORIANDER DRESSING
120ml/4fl oz/½ cup lemon juice
30ml/2 tbsp wholegrain mustard
250ml/8fl oz/1 cup olive oil
65ml/2½ fl oz/⅓ cup sesame oil
5ml/1 tsp coriander seeds, crushed
15ml/1 tbsp chopped fresh
coriander, to garnish

SERVES 6

1 Mix all the dressing ingredients in a bowl. Place the chicken breasts in a dish and pour over half the dressing. Marinate overnight in the fridge. Refrigerate the remaining dressing.

2 Cook the mangetout for 2 minutes in boiling water, then refresh in cold water. Tear the lettuces into small pieces and mix all the other salad ingredients and the bacon together. Arrange the salad on individual dishes.

3 Cook the chicken breasts on a medium barbecue for 10–15 minutes, basting with the marinade and turning once, until cooked through. Slice them on the diagonal into thin pieces. Divide between the bowls of salad and add some of the dressing to each dish. Combine quickly and scatter some fresh coriander over each bowl.

HOT AND SOUR CHICKEN SALAD

This chicken salad from Vietnam is equally delicious made with prawns.
Allow 450g/1lb fresh prawn tails to serve four people.

INGREDIENTS

2 chicken breasts, skinned and boned
115g/4oz bean sprouts
1 head Chinese leaves, shredded
2 medium carrots, cut into matchsticks
1 red onion, thinly sliced
2 large gherkins, sliced

FOR THE MARINADE
1 small red chilli, seeded and finely chopped
1cm/¹/₂in piece fresh root ginger, chopped
1 garlic clove, crushed
15ml/1 tbsp crunchy peanut butter
30ml/2 tbsp chopped fresh coriander
5ml/1 tsp sugar
2.5ml/¹/₂ tsp salt
15ml/1 tbsp rice or white wine vinegar
60ml/4 tbsp vegetable oil
10ml/2 tsp Thai fish sauce

SERVES 4–6

1 Slice the chicken breasts thinly and place in a shallow bowl. Grind the chilli, ginger and garlic in a food processor or pestle and mortar, then add the peanut butter, chopped fresh coriander, sugar and salt.

2 Add the rice or white wine vinegar, 30ml/2 tbsp of the oil and the fish sauce to the ingredients in the food processor. Combine well. Cover the chicken with the spice mixture and let marinate for at least 2–3 hours.

3 Cook the chicken on a medium-hot barbecue or in a frying pan on the hob for about 5 minutes, basting often and turning once. Arrange the salad ingredients on a serving dish and top with the cooked chicken.

CHICKEN, MUSHROOM AND CORIANDER PIZZA

Shiitake mushrooms add an earthy flavour to this colourful pizza, while fresh chilli and chilli-flavoured olive oil give it a hint of spiciness. Cook the pizza on the barbecue or in the oven.

INGREDIENTS

45ml/3 tbsp olive oil
350g/12oz skinned chicken breast fillets, cut into thin strips
1 bunch spring onions, sliced
1 fresh red chilli, seeded and chopped
1 red pepper, cut into thin strips
75g/3oz fresh shiitake mushrooms, sliced
45–60ml/3–4 tbsp chopped fresh coriander
1 pizza base, about 25–30cm/10–12in diameter
15ml/1 tbsp chilli oil
150g/5oz mozzarella cheese
salt and freshly ground black pepper

SERVES 3–4

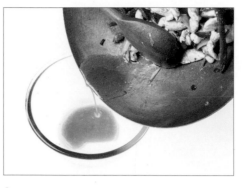

2 Pour off any excess oil, then set aside to let the chicken mixture cool.

3 Stir the fresh coriander into the cooled chicken mixture in the wok.

4 Brush all over the pizza base with the chilli oil.

5 Spoon over the chicken mixture and drizzle over the remaining olive oil.

1 Heat 30ml/2 tbsp olive oil in a wok or large frying pan. Add the chicken, spring onions, chilli, red pepper and mushrooms and stir-fry over a high heat for 2–3 minutes until the chicken is firm but still slightly pink inside. Season to taste.

6 Grate the mozzarella cheese and sprinkle it over the pizza base. Cook the pizza on a medium-hot barbecue for 15–20 minutes, until the base is crisp and golden and the cheese is bubbling. Serve the pizza immediately.

CHICKEN COOKED IN SPICES AND COCONUT

This chicken dish can be prepared in advance until you are ready to light the barbecue.
Serve the chicken with naan bread.

INGREDIENTS

200g/7oz block creamed coconut
300ml/¹/₂ pint/1¹/₄ cups boiling water
3 garlic cloves, chopped
2 spring onions, chopped
1 fresh green chilli, chopped
5cm/2in piece fresh root ginger, chopped
5ml/1 tsp fennel seeds
2.5ml/¹/₂ tsp black peppercorns
seeds from 4 cardamom pods
30ml/2 tbsp ground coriander
5ml/1 tsp ground cumin
5ml/1 tsp ground star anise
5ml/1 tsp ground nutmeg
2.5ml/¹/₂ tsp ground cloves
2.5ml/¹/₂ tsp ground turmeric
4 large chicken breasts, skinned and boned
onion rings and fresh coriander sprigs, to garnish

SERVES 4

2 Make several diagonal cuts across the chicken breasts. Arrange in a layer in a shallow dish. Spoon over half the coconut mixture and toss well to coat the chicken breasts evenly. Cover the dish and leave to marinate for at least 30 minutes, or overnight in the fridge.

3 Cook the chicken on a medium barbecue for about 12–15 minutes, turning once, until well browned and thoroughly cooked. Heat the remaining coconut mixture gently until boiling. Serve with the chicken, garnished with onion rings and sprigs of coriander.

1 Break up the coconut and put it in a jug. Pour the boiling water over and leave to dissolve. Place the chopped garlic, spring onions, chilli, ginger and all of the spices in a blender or food processor. Pour in the coconut mixture and blend to a smooth paste.

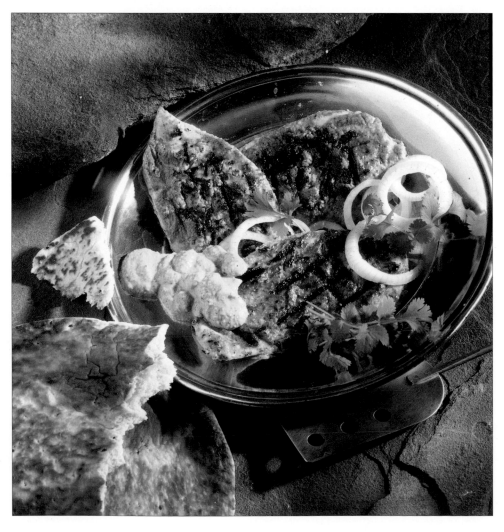

MEDITERRANEAN TURKEY SKEWERS
. . .

These attractive kebabs can be assembled in advance and left to marinate until you are ready to cook them. Barbecuing intensifies the Mediterranean flavours of the vegetables.

INGREDIENTS

2 medium courgettes
1 long thin aubergine
300g/11oz boneless turkey, cut
into 5cm/2in cubes
12–16 pickling onions
1 red or yellow pepper, cut into
5cm/2in squares

FOR THE MARINADE

90ml/6 tbsp olive oil
45ml/3 tbsp fresh lemon juice
1 garlic clove, finely chopped
30ml/2 tbsp chopped fresh basil
salt and freshly ground black
pepper

SERVES 4

3 Prepare the skewers by alternating the turkey, onions and pepper pieces. Lay the prepared skewers on a platter and sprinkle with the flavoured oil. Leave to marinate for 30 minutes.

4 Cook on a medium barbecue or under a grill for about 10 minutes, or until the turkey is cooked and the vegetables are tender, turning the skewers occasionally.

1 To make the marinade, mix the olive oil with the lemon juice, garlic and chopped fresh basil. Season well with plenty of salt and black pepper.

2 Slice the courgettes and aubergine lengthways into strips 5mm/¼ in thick. Cut them crossways about two-thirds down their length. Discard the shorter lengths. Wrap half the turkey pieces with the courgette slices and the other half with the aubergine slices.

PHEASANTS WITH SAGE AND LEMON

• • •

Pheasant is quick to cook and makes a really special summer meal.
This recipe can also be used for guinea fowl.

INGREDIENTS
2 pheasants, about 450g/1lb each
1 lemon
60ml/4 tbsp chopped fresh sage
3 shallots
5ml/1 tsp Dijon mustard
15ml/1 tbsp brandy or dry sherry
150ml/5fl oz/⅔ cup crème fraîche
salt and freshly ground black pepper
lemon wedges and sage sprigs, to garnish

SERVES 4

2 Finely grate the rind from half the lemon and slice the rest thinly. Mix together the lemon rind and half the chopped sage in a small bowl.

3 Loosen the skin on the breasts and legs of the pheasants and push a little of the sage mixture under each. Tuck the lemon slices under the skin, smoothing the skin back firmly.

4 Place the half-pheasants on a medium-hot barbecue and cook for about 25–30 minutes, turning once.

5 Meanwhile, cook the shallots on the barbecue for about 10–12 minutes, turning occasionally, until the skin is blackened and the inside very soft. Peel off the skins, chop the flesh roughly and mash it with the Dijon mustard and brandy or sherry.

6 Stir in the crème fraîche and add the reserved chopped sage. Season with plenty of salt and freshly ground black pepper. Serve the dressing with the pheasants, garnished with lemon wedges and sprigs of fresh sage.

1 Place the pheasants, breast-side upwards, on a chopping board and cut them in half lengthways, using poultry shears or a sharp kitchen knife.

Cook's Tip
Try to choose pheasants with undamaged skins, so that the flavourings stay in place during cooking.

QUAIL WITH A FIVE-SPICE MARINADE

Blending and grinding your own five-spice powder for this Vietnamese dish will give the freshest-tasting results. If you are short of time, buy a ready-mixed blend from the supermarket.

INGREDIENTS

6 quails, cleaned
2 spring onions, roughly chopped, to garnish
mandarin orange or satsuma, to garnish
banana leaves, to serve

FOR THE MARINADE
2 pieces star anise
10ml/2 tsp ground cinnamon
10ml/2 tsp fennel seeds
10ml/2 tsp Sichuan pepper
a pinch ground cloves
1 small onion, finely chopped
1 garlic clove, crushed
60ml/4 tbsp clear honey
30ml/2 tbsp dark soy sauce

SERVES 4–6

1 Remove the backbones from the quails by cutting down either side with a pair of strong kitchen scissors.

2 Flatten the birds with the palm of your hand and secure each bird using two bamboo skewers.

3 To make the marinade, place the five spices in a pestle and mortar or spice mill and grind into a fine powder. Add the chopped onion, garlic, clear honey and soy sauce, and combine until thoroughly mixed.

4 Arrange the quails on a flat dish and pour over the marinade. Cover with clear film and leave in the fridge for 8 hours or overnight for the flavours to mingle.

5 Cook the quails on a medium barbecue for 15–20 minutes until golden brown, basting occasionally with the marinade and turning once.

6 To garnish, remove the outer zest from the mandarin orange or satsuma, using a vegetable peeler. Shred the zest finely and combine with the chopped spring onions. Arrange the quails on a bed of banana leaves and garnish with the orange zest and spring onions.

Cook's Tip
If you prefer, or if quails are not available, you could use other poultry such as poussins as a substitute.

Fish and Seafood

Cooking over charcoal adds a marvellous flavour to fish and seafood, and it's very quick and easy to prepare this way. Oily fish such as mackerel, sardines or tuna are perfectly suited to grilling and won't dry out, while chargrilling will enhance their robust flavours. Use plump prawns or firm meaty-textured fish such as monkfish for kebabs, but marinate them first to keep them moist. More delicate fish, or those that are best cooked in their own steam, can also be barbecued very successfully: just wrap them securely in foil and cook them either on the rack or directly on the coals. You can include all kinds of flavourings in the foil parcels, too.

TIGER PRAWN SKEWERS WITH WALNUT PESTO

∘ ∘ ∘

This is an unusual starter or main course, which can be prepared in advance and kept in the fridge until you're ready to cook it.

INGREDIENTS

12–16 large, raw, shell-on tiger prawns
50g/2oz/½ cup walnut pieces
60ml/4 tbsp chopped fresh flat-leaf parsley
60ml/4 tbsp chopped fresh basil
2 garlic cloves, chopped
45ml/3 tbsp grated fresh Parmesan cheese
30ml/2 tbsp extra virgin olive oil
30ml/2 tbsp walnut oil
salt and freshly ground black pepper

SERVES 4

3 Add half the pesto to the prawns in the bowl, toss them well, then cover and chill in the fridge for a minimum of 1 hour, or leave them overnight.

4 Thread the prawns on to skewers and cook them on a hot barbecue for 3–4 minutes, turning once. Serve with the remaining pesto and a green salad.

1 Peel the prawns, removing the head but leaving the tail. De-vein and then put the prawns in a large mixing bowl.

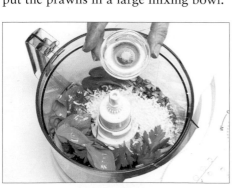

2 To make the pesto, place the walnuts, parsley, basil, garlic, cheese and oils in a food processor and process until finely chopped. Season.

SPICED PRAWNS WITH VEGETABLES

· · ·

*This is a light and nutritious Indian dish, excellent served either on a bed of lettuce leaves,
or with plain boiled rice or chappatis.*

INGREDIENTS

20 cooked king prawns, peeled
1 medium courgette, thickly sliced
1 medium onion, cut into 8 chunks
8 cherry tomatoes
8 baby corn cobs
mixed salad leaves, to serve

FOR THE MARINADE
30ml/2 tbsp chopped fresh
coriander
5ml/1 tsp salt
2 fresh green chillies, seeded if
wished
45ml/3 tbsp lemon juice
30ml/2 tbsp vegetable oil

SERVES 4

1 To make the marinade, blend the coriander, salt, chillies, lemon juice and oil together in a food processor.

2 Empty the contents from the processor and transfer to a bowl.

3 Add the peeled king prawns to the mixture in the bowl and stir to make sure that all the prawns are well coated. Cover the bowl with clear film and set aside in a cool place, to marinate for about 30 minutes.

4 Arrange the vegetables and prawns alternately on four long skewers. Cook on a medium barbecue for 5 minutes, turning frequently, until cooked and browned. Serve immediately, on a bed of mixed salad leaves.

CALAMARI WITH TWO-TOMATO STUFFING

*Calamari, or baby squid, are quick to cook, but do turn and baste them often
and take care not to overcook them.*

INGREDIENTS

*500g/1¼ lb baby squid, cleaned
1 garlic clove, crushed
3 plum tomatoes, skinned and
chopped
8 sun-dried tomatoes in oil,
drained and chopped
60ml/4 tbsp chopped fresh basil,
plus extra, to serve
60ml/4 tbsp fresh white
breadcrumbs
45ml/3 tbsp olive oil
15ml/1 tbsp red wine vinegar
salt and freshly ground black
pepper
lemon juice, to serve*

SERVES 4

1 Remove the tentacles from the squid and roughly chop them; leave the main part of the squid whole.

2 Mix together the crushed garlic, plum tomatoes, sun-dried tomatoes, chopped fresh basil and breadcrumbs. Stir in 15ml/1 tbsp of the olive oil and the vinegar. Season well with plenty of salt and freshly ground black pepper. Soak some wooden cocktail sticks in water for 10 minutes before use, to prevent them burning on the barbecue.

3 Using a teaspoon, fill the squid with the stuffing mixture. Secure the open ends with the cocktail sticks to hold the stuffing mixture in place.

4 Brush the squid with the remaining olive oil and cook over a medium-hot barbecue for 4–5 minutes, turning often. Sprinkle with lemon juice and extra chopped fresh basil to serve.

SARDINES WITH WARM HERB SALSA

. . .

Plain grilling is the very best way to cook fresh sardines. Served with this luscious herb salsa the only other essential item is fresh, crusty bread, to mop up the tasty juices.

INGREDIENTS

12–16 fresh sardines
oil for brushing
juice of 1 lemon

FOR THE SALSA
15ml/1 tbsp butter
4 spring onions, chopped
1 garlic clove, finely chopped
rind of 1 lemon
30ml/2 tbsp finely chopped fresh
parsley
30ml/2 tbsp finely snipped fresh
chives
30ml/2 tbsp finely chopped fresh
basil
30ml/2 tbsp green olive paste
10ml/2 tsp balsamic vinegar
salt and freshly ground black
pepper

SERVES 4

1 To clean the sardines, use a pair of small kitchen scissors to slit the fish along the belly and pull out the innards. Wipe the fish with kitchen paper and then arrange on a grill rack.

2 To make the salsa, melt the butter in a small pan and gently sauté the spring onions and garlic for about 2 minutes, shaking the pan occasionally, until softened but not browned.

3 Add the lemon rind and remaining salsa ingredients to the onions and garlic in the pan and keep warm on the edge of the barbecue, stirring occasionally. Do not allow to boil.

4 Brush the sardines lightly with oil and sprinkle with lemon juice, salt and pepper. Cook for about 2 minutes on each side, over a moderate heat. Serve with the warm salsa and crusty bread.

CHAR-GRILLED TUNA WITH FIERY PEPPER PUREE

. . .

Tuna is an oily fish that barbecues well and is meaty enough to combine successfully with strong flavours – even hot chilli, as in this red pepper purée, which is excellent served with crusty bread.

INGREDIENTS

4 tuna steaks, about 175g/6oz each
finely grated rind and juice of 1 lime
30ml/2 tbsp olive oil
salt and freshly ground black pepper
lime wedges, to serve

FOR THE PEPPER PURÉE
2 red peppers, halved
45ml/3 tbsp olive oil, plus extra for brushing
1 small onion
2 garlic cloves, crushed
2 red chillies
1 slice white bread without crusts, diced
salt

SERVES 4

2 To make the pepper purée, brush the pepper halves with a little olive oil and cook them, skin-side down, on a hot barbecue, until the skin is charred and blackened. Place the onion in its skin on the barbecue and cook until browned, turning it occasionally.

4 Place the cooked peppers and onion with the garlic, chillies, bread and olive oil in a food processor. Process until smooth. Add salt to taste.

3 Leave the peppers and onion until cool enough to handle, then remove the skins, using a sharp kitchen knife.

5 Drain the tuna steaks from the marinade and cook them on a hot barbecue for 8–10 minutes, turning once, until golden brown. Serve the steaks with the pepper purée and lime wedges, with crusty bread if liked.

1 Trim any skin from the tuna and place the steaks in a single layer in a wide dish. Sprinkle over the lime rind and juice, olive oil, salt and black pepper. Cover with clear film and chill in the fridge until required.

Cook's Tip

The pepper purée can be made in advance, cooking the peppers and onion under a hot grill; keep it in the fridge until you cook the fish.

MACKEREL KEBABS WITH SWEET PEPPER SALAD

Mackerel is an excellent fish for barbecuing because its natural oils keep it moist and tasty. This recipe combines mackerel with peppers and tomatoes in a flavoursome summer salad.

INGREDIENTS

4 medium mackerel, about
225g/8oz each, filleted
2 small red onions, cut in wedges
30ml/2 tbsp chopped fresh
marjoram
60ml/4 tbsp dry white wine
45ml/3 tbsp olive oil
juice of 1 lime

FOR THE SALAD

1 red pepper
1 yellow pepper
1 small red onion
2 large plum tomatoes
15ml/1 tbsp chopped fresh
marjoram
10ml/2 tsp balsamic vinegar
salt and freshly ground black
pepper

SERVES 4

2 Mix together the marjoram, wine, oil and lime juice and spoon over the mackerel. Cover and chill in the fridge for at least 30 minutes, turning once.

3 To make the salad, quarter and seed both peppers and halve the onion. Place the peppers and onion, skin-side down, with the whole tomatoes, on a hot barbecue and leave until the skins are blackened and charred.

5 Chop the vegetables roughly and put them in a bowl. Stir in the marjoram and balsamic vinegar and season to taste. Toss thoroughly.

6 Remove the kebabs from the fridge and cook on a hot barbecue for about 10–12 minutes, turning occasionally and basting with the marinade. Serve with the pepper salad.

1 Thread each mackerel fillet on to a skewer, with an onion wedge on each end. Arrange the skewers in a dish.

4 Remove the vegetables from the barbecue and leave until they are cool enough to handle. Use a sharp knife to peel off and discard the skins.

Cook's Tip

Other oily fish can be used for this dish: try fillets or cubes of herring, rainbow trout or salmon, instead.

BARBECUED SCALLOPS WITH LIME BUTTER

. . .

Fresh scallops are quick to cook and ideal for barbecues. This recipe combines them simply with lime and fennel.

INGREDIENTS

1 head fennel

2 limes

12 large scallops, cleaned

1 egg yolk

90ml/6 tbsp melted butter

olive oil for brushing

salt and freshly ground

black pepper

SERVES 4

3 Place the egg yolk and remaining lime rind and juice in a small bowl and whisk until pale and smooth.

5 Brush the fennel wedges with olive oil and cook them on a hot barbecue for 3–4 minutes, turning once.

1 Trim any feathery leaves from the fennel and reserve them. Slice the rest lengthways into thin wedges.

4 Gradually whisk in the melted butter and continue whisking until thick and smooth. Finely chop the reserved fennel leaves and stir them in, with seasoning to taste.

6 Add the scallops and cook for a further 3–4 minutes, turning once. Serve with the lime and fennel butter and the lime wedges.

2 Cut one lime into wedges. Finely grate the rind and squeeze the juice of the other lime and toss half the juice and rind on to the scallops. Season well with salt and fresh black pepper.

Cook's Tip

If the scallops are small, you may wish to thread them on to flat skewers to make turning them easier.

TROUT WITH BACON

• • •

*The smoky, savoury flavour of crispy grilled bacon perfectly complements
the delicate flesh of the trout in this simple dish.*

INGREDIENTS

4 trout, cleaned and gutted
25g/1oz/1 tbsp plain flour
4 rashers smoked streaky bacon
30ml/2 tbsp olive oil
juice of ½ lemon
salt and freshly ground
black pepper

SERVES 4

1 Place the trout on a chopping
board and pat dry with kitchen paper.
Season the flour with the salt and
freshly ground black pepper. Stretch
the bacon rashers out thinly using the
back of a heavy kitchen knife.

2 Roll the fish in the seasoned flour
mixture and wrap tightly in the streaky
bacon. Brush with olive oil and cook
on a medium-hot barbecue for 10–15
minutes, turning once. Serve at once,
with the lemon juice drizzled on top.

MACKEREL WITH TOMATOES, PESTO AND ONION
. . .

Rich oily fish like mackerel needs a sharp, fresh-tasting sauce to go with it,
and this aromatic pesto is excellent drizzled over the top.

INGREDIENTS

4 mackerel, cleaned and gutted
30ml/2 tbsp olive oil
115g/4oz onion, roughly chopped
450g/1lb tomatoes, roughly
chopped
salt and freshly ground
black pepper

FOR THE PESTO
50g/2oz pine nuts
30ml/2 tbsp fresh basil leaves
2 garlic cloves, crushed
30ml/2 tbsp freshly grated
Parmesan cheese
150ml/¼ pint/⅔ cup extra virgin
olive oil

SERVES 4

1 To make the pesto, place the pine nuts, fresh basil leaves and garlic in a food processor and blend to a rough paste. Add the Parmesan and, with the blades running, gradually add the oil.

2 Season the mackerel well with plenty of salt and freshly ground black pepper and cook on a medium-hot barbecue for about 12–15 minutes, turning once.

3 Meanwhile, heat the olive oil in a large, heavy-based saucepan and sauté the chopped onions until soft and golden brown.

4 Stir the chopped tomatoes into the contents of the saucepan and cook for 5 minutes. Serve the fish on top of the tomato mixture and top with a generous spoonful of the pesto.

MONKFISH WITH PEPPERED CITRUS MARINADE

Monkfish is a firm, meaty fish that cooks well on the barbecue and keeps its shape.
Serve with a green salad.

INGREDIENTS

2 monkfish tails, about
350g/12oz each
1 lime
1 lemon
2 oranges
handful of fresh thyme sprigs
30ml/2 tbsp olive oil
15ml/1 tbsp mixed peppercorns,
roughly crushed
salt and freshly ground
black pepper

SERVES 4

2 Turn the fish and repeat on the other side, to remove the second fillet. Repeat on the second tail. (If you prefer, you can ask your fishmonger to do this for you.) Lay the four fillets out flat on a chopping board.

5 Squeeze the juice from the citrus fruits and mix it with the olive oil and more salt and pepper. Spoon over the fish. Cover with clear film and leave to marinate in the fridge for about 1 hour, turning occasionally and spooning the marinade over the fish.

1 Using a sharp kitchen knife, remove any skin from the monkfish tails. Cut carefully down one side of the backbone, sliding the knife between the bone and flesh, to remove the fillet on one side.

3 Cut two slices from each of the citrus fruits and arrange them over two of the fillets. Add a few sprigs of fresh thyme and sprinkle with plenty of salt and freshly ground black pepper. Finely grate the rind from the remaining fruit and sprinkle it over the fish.

6 Drain the monkfish, reserving the marinade, and sprinkle with the crushed peppercorns. Cook on a medium-hot barbecue for 15–20 minutes, basting with the marinade and turning occasionally, until the fish is evenly cooked.

4 Lay the other two fillets on top and tie them firmly at intervals.

FISH PARCELS

○ ● ○

*Sea bass is good for this recipe, but you could also use small whole trout
or a white fish fillet such as cod or haddock.*

INGREDIENTS

*4 pieces sea bass fillet, or 4 small
sea bass, about 450g/1lb each
olive oil for brushing
2 shallots, thinly sliced
1 garlic clove, chopped
15ml/1 tbsp capers
6 sun-dried tomatoes, finely
chopped
4 black olives, stoned and thinly
sliced
grated rind and juice of 1 lemon
5ml/1 tsp paprika
salt and freshly ground black
pepper*

SERVES 4

2 Place a piece of fish in the centre
of each piece of baking foil and season
well with plenty of salt and pepper.

3 Scatter over the shallots, chopped
garlic, capers, tomatoes, sliced olives
and grated lemon rind. Sprinkle with
the lemon juice and paprika.

4 Fold over the baking foil to enclose
the fish loosely, sealing the edges firmly
so that none of the juices can escape
during cooking. Place the parcels on a
moderately hot barbecue and cook for
about 8–10 minutes. To serve, place
each of the parcels on a plate and
loosen the tops to open.

Cook's Tip
These parcels can also be
baked in the oven: place them
on a baking sheet and cook at
200°C/400°F/Gas 6 for
about 15–20 minutes.

1 Clean the fish if whole. Cut four
squares of double-thickness baking foil,
large enough to enclose the fish; brush
lightly with a little olive oil.

MEXICO BARBECUED SALMON

· · ·

The sauce for this dish is vibrant with hot, sweet and sour flavours that permeate the fish before and during cooking.

INGREDIENTS

1 small red onion
1 garlic clove
6 plum tomatoes
25g/1oz/2 tbsp butter
45ml/3 tbsp tomato ketchup
30ml/2 tbsp Dijon mustard
30ml/2 tbsp dark brown sugar
15ml/1 tbsp runny honey
5ml/1 tbsp cayenne pepper
15ml/1 tbsp ancho chilli powder
15ml/1 tbsp paprika
15ml/1 tbsp Worcestershire sauce
4 salmon fillets, about 175g/6oz
each

SERVES 4

3 Melt the butter in a large, heavy-based saucepan and gently cook the onion and garlic until translucent.

4 Add the tomatoes to the saucepan and allow to simmer for 15 minutes.

5 Add the remaining ingredients, excluding the salmon, and simmer for a further 20 minutes. Pour the mixture into a food processor and blend until smooth. Leave to cool.

1 Using a sharp knife, finely chop the red onion and finely dice the garlic.

2 Next, dice the plum tomatoes finely and set them aside.

6 Brush the salmon with the sauce, and chill for at least 2 hours. Cook on a hot barbecue for 6 minutes, basting with the sauce and turning once.

Vegetarian Dishes and Vegetables

Vegetables cooked on the barbecue acquire a richness and depth

of flavour that will add an extra dimension to your meal. There are

lots of ideas here for vegetable accompaniments to meat and fish dishes,

as well as for substantial main dishes that everyone, vegetarian or not,

will love. All vegetables can be cooked in foil parcels, but many are

ideally suited to grilling on the barbecue: jacket potatoes, peppers,

aubergines and corn on the cob are irresistible cooked over charcoal,

or you can spear a mixture of vegetables on to skewers to make

colourful and delicious kebabs. Barbecued vegetables can also be cooled

and made into fabulous salads. They certainly shouldn't be

an afterthought on your barbecue menu.

GRILLED AUBERGINE PARCELS

These little Italian bundles of tomatoes, mozzarella cheese and basil, wrapped in slices of aubergine, taste delicious cooked on the barbecue.

INGREDIENTS

2 large, long aubergines
225g/8oz mozzarella cheese
2 plum tomatoes
16 large fresh basil leaves
30ml/2 tbsp olive oil
salt and freshly ground black pepper

FOR THE DRESSING
60ml/4 tbsp olive oil
5ml/1 tsp balsamic vinegar
15ml/1 tbsp sun-dried tomato paste
15ml/1 tbsp lemon juice

FOR THE GARNISH
30ml/2 tbsp toasted pine nuts
torn fresh basil leaves

SERVES 4

3 Cut the mozzarella cheese into eight slices. Cut each tomato into eight slices, not counting the first and last slices. Take two aubergine slices and arrange in a cross. Place a slice of tomato in the centre, season, then add a basil leaf, followed by a slice of mozzarella, another basil leaf, another slice of tomato and more seasoning.

4 Fold the ends of the aubergine slices around the filling to make a neat parcel. Repeat with the rest of the assembled ingredients to make eight parcels. Chill the parcels in the fridge for about 20 minutes.

5 To make the tomato dressing, whisk together the olive oil, vinegar, sun-dried tomato paste and lemon juice. Season to taste with plenty of salt and freshly ground black pepper.

1 Remove the stalks from the aubergines and cut them lengthways into thin slices using a mandolin or long-bladed knife – aim to get 16 slices in total, each about 5mm/¼in thick, disregarding the first and last slices.

2 Bring a large saucepan of salted water to the boil and cook the aubergine slices for about 2 minutes, until just softened. Drain the slices, then pat them dry on kitchen paper.

6 Brush the parcels with olive oil and cook on a hot barbecue for about 10 minutes, turning once, until golden. Serve hot, with the dressing, sprinkled with pine nuts and basil.

VEGETABLE PARCELS WITH FLOWERY BUTTER

° ° °

Nasturtium leaves and flowers are edible and have a distinctive peppery flavour.
They make a pretty addition to summer barbecue dishes.

INGREDIENTS

200g/7oz baby carrots
250g/9oz yellow patty-pan
squashes or yellow courgettes
115g/4oz baby sweetcorn
1 onion, thinly sliced
50g/2oz/4 tbsp butter, plus extra
for greasing
finely grated rind of ½ lemon
6 young nasturtium leaves
4–8 nasturtium flowers
salt and freshly ground
black pepper

SERVES 4

1 Trim the vegetables with a sharp knife, leaving them whole unless they are very large – if necessary, cut them into even-size pieces.

2 Divide the vegetables between four double-thickness squares of buttered baking foil and season well.

3 Mix the butter with the lemon rind in a small bowl. Roughly chop the nasturtium leaves and add them to the butter. Place a generous spoonful of the butter on each pile of vegetables in the squares of baking foil.

4 Fold over the foil and seal the edges to make a neat parcel. Cook on a medium-hot barbecue for 30 minutes until the vegetables are tender. Open the parcels and top each with one or two nasturtium flowers. Serve at once.

SPINACH WITH RAISINS AND PINE NUTS

Raisins and pine nuts are frequent partners in Spanish recipes. In this recipe they are tossed with wilted spinach and croûtons, and can be cooked quickly in a flameproof pan on the barbecue.

INGREDIENTS

50g/2oz/⅓ cup raisins
1 thick slice crusty white bread
45ml/3 tbsp olive oil
25g/1oz/⅓ cup pine nuts
500g/1¼ lb young spinach, stalks removed
2 garlic cloves, crushed
salt and freshly ground black pepper

SERVES 4

1 Put the raisins in a bowl, cover with boiling water and leave to soak for 10 minutes. Drain and set aside.

2 Cut the bread into cubes and discard the crusts. Heat 30ml/2 tbsp of the olive oil in a large frying pan and fry the bread until golden brown.

3 Heat the remaining oil and fry the pine nuts, on the barbecue or hob, until beginning to colour. Add the spinach and garlic and cook quickly, turning the spinach until it has just wilted. Toss in the raisins and season lightly with salt and pepper. Transfer to a serving dish. Scatter with croûtons and serve.

BAKED STUFFED COURGETTES

° ° °

The tangy goat's cheese stuffing contrasts well with the very delicate flavour of the courgettes in this recipe. Wrap the courgettes and bake them in the embers of the fire.

2 Insert pieces of goat's cheese in the slits. Add a little chopped mint and sprinkle over the oil and black pepper.

3 Wrap each courgette in foil, place in the embers of the fire and bake for about 25 minutes, until tender.

INGREDIENTS

8 small courgettes, about
450g/1lb total weight
15ml/1 tbsp olive oil, plus
extra for brushing
75–115g/3–4oz goat's cheese,
cut into thin strips
a few sprigs of fresh mint,
finely chopped, plus extra
to garnish
freshly ground black pepper

SERVES 4

1 Cut eight pieces of baking foil large enough to encase each courgette, and lightly brush each piece with olive oil. Trim the courgettes and cut a thin slit along the length of each.

Cook's Tip

While almost any cheese can be used in this recipe, mild cheeses such as Cheddar or mozzarella, will best allow the flavour of the courgettes to be appreciated.

SWEETCORN IN A GARLIC BUTTER CRUST

Whether you are catering for vegetarians or serving this with meat dishes, it will disappear in a flash. The charred garlic butter crust adds a new dimension to the corn cobs.

INGREDIENTS

6 ripe corn cobs
225g/8oz/1 cup butter
30ml/2 tbsp olive oil
2 garlic cloves, crushed
115g/4oz/1 cup wholemeal
breadcrumbs
15ml/1 tbsp chopped fresh parsley
salt and freshly ground black
pepper

SERVES 6

1 Pull off the husks and silks and boil the corn cobs in a large saucepan of salted water until tender. Drain the corn cobs and leave to cool.

2 Melt the butter in a saucepan and add the olive oil, crushed garlic, salt and freshly ground black pepper, and stir to blend. Pour the mixture into a shallow dish. In another shallow dish blend the breadcrumbs and chopped fresh parsley. Roll the corn cobs in the melted butter mixture and then in the breadcrumbs until they are well coated.

3 Cook the corn cobs on a hot barbecue for about 10 minutes, turning frequently, until the breadcrumbs are golden brown.

BAKED SQUASH WITH PARMESAN

Almost all types of squash are suitable for barbecue cooking, and they are extemely easy to deal with: simply wrap them in baking foil and place them in the hot embers until they soften.

INGREDIENTS

2 acorn or butternut squashes,
about 450g/1lb each
15ml/1 tbsp olive oil
50g/2oz/4 tbsp butter, melted
75g/3oz/1 cup grated Parmesan
cheese
60ml/4 tbsp pine nuts, toasted
salt and freshly ground black
pepper
2.5ml/1/2 tsp freshly grated nutmeg

SERVES 4

2 Brush the cut surfaces with oil and sprinkle with salt and black pepper.

3 Wrap each squash in baking foil and place in the embers of the fire. Cook for 25–30 minutes, until tender. Turn the parcels occasionally so that the squash cook evenly.

5 Dice the flesh, then stir in the melted butter. Add the Parmesan, pine nuts, salt and pepper. Toss well to mix.

6 Spoon the mixture back into the shells. Sprinkle with nutmeg to serve.

1 Cut the squashes in half and scoop out the seeds with a spoon.

4 Leave the squash until cool enough to handle. Unwrap the squashes from the foil parcels and scoop out the flesh, leaving the skins intact.

Cook's Tip

Spaghetti squash can also be cooked in this way. Just scoop out the spaghetti-like strands and toss with butter and Parmesan cheese.

SUMMER VEGETABLES WITH YOGURT PESTO

• • •

*Char-grilled vegetables make a meal on their own, or are delicious served as a
Mediterranean-style accompaniment to grilled meats and fish.*

INGREDIENTS

2 small aubergines
2 large courgettes
1 red pepper
1 yellow pepper
1 fennel bulb
1 red onion
olive oil, for brushing
salt and freshly ground black
pepper

FOR THE YOGURT PESTO
150ml/¼ pint/⅔ cup Greek-style
yogurt
45ml/3 tbsp pesto

SERVES 4

2 Use a sharp kitchen knife to cut
the courgettes in half lengthways. Cut
the peppers in half, removing the seeds
but leaving the stalks in place.

5 Arrange the vegetables on the hot
barbecue, brush generously with olive
oil and sprinkle with plenty of salt and
freshly ground black pepper.

3 Slice the fennel bulb and the red
onion into thick wedges, using a sharp
kitchen knife.

6 Cook the vegetables until golden
brown and tender, turning occasionally.
The aubergines and peppers will take
6–8 minutes to cook, the courgettes,
onion and fennel 4–5 minutes. Serve
the vegetables as soon as they are
cooked, with the yogurt pesto.

1 Cut the aubergines into 1cm/½in
slices. Sprinkle with salt and leave to
drain for about 30 minutes. Rinse well
in cold running water and pat dry.

4 Stir the yogurt and pesto lightly
together in a bowl, to make a marbled
sauce. Spoon the yogurt pesto into a
serving bowl and set aside.

Cook's Tip
Baby vegetables make
excellent candidates for grilling
whole, so look out for baby
aubergines and peppers, in
particular. There's no need to
salt the aubergines if they're small.

POTATO SKEWERS WITH MUSTARD DIP

· · ·

Potatoes cooked on the barbecue have a tasty flavour and crisp skin.
These skewers are served with a thick, garlic-rich dip.

INGREDIENTS

1kg/2¼lb small new potatoes
200g/7oz/2 cups shallots, halved
30ml/2 tbsp olive oil
15ml/1 tbsp sea salt

FOR THE MUSTARD DIP
4 garlic cloves, crushed
2 egg yolks
30ml/2 tbsp lemon juice
300ml/½ pint/1¼ cups extra
virgin olive oil
10ml/2 tsp whole-grain mustard
salt and freshly ground black
pepper

SERVES 4

1 To make the mustard dip, place the garlic, egg yolks and lemon juice in a blender or food processor and process for a few seconds until smooth.

2 With the motor running, add the oil, until the mixture forms a thick cream. Add the mustard and season.

3 Par-boil the potatoes in salted boiling water for about 5 minutes. Drain well and then thread them on to metal skewers with the shallots.

4 Brush with olive oil and sprinkle with sea salt. Cook for 10–12 minutes over a hot barbecue, turning often, until tender. Serve with the mustard dip.

POTATO WEDGES WITH GARLIC AND ROSEMARY

· · ·

Toss the potato wedges in fragrant, garlicky olive oil with chopped fresh rosemary before barbecuing them over the coals.

INGREDIENTS

675g/1½ lb medium old potatoes
15ml/1 tbsp olive oil
2 garlic cloves, thinly sliced
60ml/4 tbsp chopped fresh rosemary
salt and freshly ground black pepper

SERVES 4

1 Cut each potato into four wedges and par-boil in boiling salted water for 5 minutes. Drain well.

2 Toss the potatoes in the olive oil with the garlic, rosemary and black pepper. Arrange on a grill rack.

3 Cook the potatoes on a hot barbecue for about 15 minutes, turning occasionally, until the wedges are crisp and golden brown.

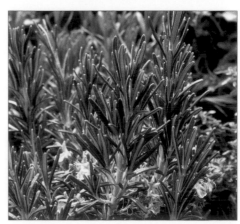

Salads and Accompaniments

Cool salads are a perfect foil to barbecued food, but they

should have assertive characters of their own. The recipes that

follow include some marvellous sunny, Mediterranean flavours that

taste especially good on summer days, and a selection of them would

be perfect as part of a buffet for a party. Don't forget that you can use

the barbecue to grill ingredients such as tomatoes, peppers, aubergines

and radicchio – it will give them an intense, smoky flavour that

will pervade the whole salad.

SALSAS, DIPS AND MARINADES

———◆———

The powerful flavours of barbecued meat and fish call for spicy,

lively accompaniments. Chunky salsas are ideal, with their

intriguing combination of cool, crisp ingredients and fiery flavours.

Tangy barbecue sauce is a more traditional alternative that children

adore. For a subtler effect, melt a pat of butter flavoured with herbs,

garlic or anchovies over a plainly grilled steak or fish. This chapter

also includes some appetizing dips to go with crisps, bread sticks

and crudités, and a selection of delicious marinades suitable for

a wide variety of meat and fish.

DESSERTS

—⟫◆⟪—

At the end of a barbecue it's a lovely idea to use the lingering fire

to make a delicious fruity dessert. You can cook fruit to melting

tenderness by wrapping it in foil, including sugar, spices and a sprinkling

of liqueur in the parcel. To grill fruit, cut it into chunks and spear it

on skewers, or just lay large slices on the grill rack. Sprinkle it with

sugar to caramelize in the heat. The aroma is intoxicating: even those

who thought they couldn't eat another bite will be beguiled by it.

Accompany barbecued fruit with a buttery, spicy sauce, crisp toasted

brioche or freshly made griddle cakes – and perhaps a scoop of whipped

cream or ice cream – to make a perfect end to the meal.

CHARGRILLED APPLES ON CINNAMON TOASTS

* * *

This simple, scrumptious dessert is best made with an enriched bread such as brioche,
but any light sweet bread will do.

INGREDIENTS

4 sweet, dessert apples
juice of ½ lemon
4 individual brioches or muffins
60ml/4 tbsp melted butter
30ml/2 tbsp golden caster sugar
5ml/1 tsp ground cinnamon
whipped cream or Greek-style
yogurt, to serve

SERVES 4

2 Cut the brioches or muffins into thick slices. Brush the slices with melted butter on both sides.

4 Place the apple and brioche slices on a medium-hot barbecue and cook them for about 3–4 minutes, turning once, until they are beginning to turn golden brown. Do not allow to burn.

1 Core the apples and use a sharp knife to cut them into 3–4 thick slices. Sprinkle the apple slices with lemon juice and set them aside.

3 Mix together the caster sugar and ground cinnamon in a small bowl to make the cinnamon sugar. Set aside.

5 Sprinkle half the cinnamon sugar over the apple slices and brioche toasts and cook for a further minute on the barbecue, until the sugar is sizzling and the toasts are a rich golden brown.

6 To serve, arrange the apple slices over the toasts and sprinkle them with the remaining cinnamon sugar. Serve hot, with whipped cream or Greek-style yogurt, if liked.

PINEAPPLE WEDGES WITH RUM BUTTER GLAZE
. . .

Fresh pineapple is even more full of flavour when barbecued, and this spiced rum glaze makes it into a very special dessert.

INGREDIENTS

1 medium pineapple
30ml/2 tbsp dark muscovado sugar
5ml/1 tsp ground ginger
60ml/4 tbsp melted butter
30ml/2 tbsp dark rum

SERVES 4

3 Soak 4 bamboo skewers in water for 15 minutes to prevent them scorching on the barbecue. Push a skewer through each wedge, into the stalk, to hold the chunks in place.

4 Mix together the sugar, ginger, butter and rum and brush over the pineapple. Cook the wedges on the barbecue for 4 minutes; pour the remaining glaze over the top and serve.

1 With a large, sharp knife, cut the pineapple lengthways into four wedges. Cut out and discard the central core.

2 Cut between the flesh and skin, to release the skin, but leave the flesh in place. Slice the flesh across and lengthways to make thick chunks.

Cook's Tip

For an easier version, simply remove the skin and then cut the whole pineapple into thick slices and cook as above.

BAKED BANANAS WITH SPICY VANILLA FILLING

Bananas are ideal for barbecue cooking as they bake in their skins and need no preparation at all. This flavoured butter adds richness; children may prefer melted chocolate, jam or honey.

INGREDIENTS

4 bananas
6 green cardamom pods
1 vanilla pod
finely grated rind of 1 small orange
30ml/2 tbsp brandy or orange juice
60ml/4 tbsp light muscovado sugar
45ml/3 tbsp butter
crème fraîche or Greek-style
yogurt, to serve

SERVES 4

1 Place the bananas, in their skins, on a hot barbecue and leave for 6–8 minutes, turning occasionally, until they are turning brownish-black.

2 Meanwhile, split the cardamom pods and remove the seeds. Crush lightly in a pestle and mortar.

3 Split the vanilla pod lengthways and scrape out the tiny seeds. Mix with the cardamom seeds, orange rind, brandy or juice, muscovado sugar and butter into a thick paste.

4 Using a sharp knife, slit the skin of each banana, then open out the skin and spoon in a little of the paste. Serve with a spoonful of crème fraîche or Greek-style yogurt, if liked.

ORANGES IN MAPLE AND COINTREAU SYRUP

*This is one of the most delicious ways to eat an orange, and a luxurious way to round off
a barbecued meal. For a children's or alcohol-free version, omit the liqueur.*

INGREDIENTS

20ml/4 tsp butter, plus extra,
melted, for brushing
4 medium oranges
30 ml/2 tbsp maple syrup
30ml/2 tbsp Cointreau or Grand
Marnier liqueur
crème fraîche or fromage frais,
to serve

SERVES 4

2 Remove some shreds of orange rind, to decorate. Blanch these, dry them and set them aside. Peel the oranges, removing all the white pith and catching the juice in a bowl.

3 Slice the oranges crossways into thick slices. Reassemble them and place each orange on a square of baking foil.

4 Tuck the baking foil up securely around the oranges to keep them in shape, leaving the foil open at the top.

5 Mix together the reserved orange juice, maple syrup and liqueur and spoon the mixture over the oranges.

6 Add a knob of butter to each parcel and close the foil at the top to seal in the juices. Place the parcels on a hot barbecue for 10–12 minutes, until hot. Serve with crème fraîche or fromage frais, topped with the reserved shreds of orange rind.

1 Cut four double-thickness squares of baking foil, large enough to wrap each of the oranges. Brush the centre of each square of foil with plenty of melted butter.

GRIDDLE CAKES WITH MULLED PLUMS

· · ·

These delectably light little pancakes are fun to make on the barbecue. They are served with a rich, spicy plum sauce.

INGREDIENTS

500g/1¼ lb red plums
90ml/6 tbsp light muscovado sugar
1 cinnamon stick
2 whole cloves
1 piece star anise
90ml/6 tbsp apple juice
cream or Greek-style yogurt,
to serve

FOR THE GRIDDLE CAKES

50g/2oz/½ cup plain flour
10ml/2 tsp baking powder
pinch of salt
50g/2oz/½ cup fine cornmeal
30ml/2 tbsp light muscovado sugar
1 egg, beaten
300ml/½ pint/1¼ cups milk
30ml/2 tbsp corn oil

SERVES 6

1 Halve, stone and quarter the plums. Place them in a flameproof pan, with the sugar, spices and apple juice.

Cook's Tip

If you prefer, make the griddle cakes in advance, on the hob, and then simply heat them for a few seconds on the barbecue to serve with the plums.

2 Bring to the boil, then reduce the heat, cover the pan and simmer gently for 8–10 minutes, stirring occasionally, until the plums are soft. Remove the spices and keep the plums warm on the side of the barbecue.

3 For the griddle cakes, sift the plain flour, baking powder and salt into a large mixing bowl and stir in the cornmeal and muscovado sugar.

4 Make a well in the centre of the ingredients and add the egg, then beat in the milk. Beat thoroughly with a whisk or wooden spoon to form a smooth batter. Beat in half the oil.

5 Heat a griddle or a heavy frying pan on a hot barbecue. Brush with the remaining oil, then drop tablespoons of batter on to it, allowing them to spread. Cook the griddle cakes for about a minute, until bubbles start to appear on the surface and the underside is golden brown.

6 Turn the cakes over and cook the other side for a further minute, or until golden. Serve the cakes hot from the griddle with a spoonful of mulled plums and cream or yogurt.

FRUIT KEBABS WITH CHOCOLATE FONDUE
. . .

Fondues are always lots of fun, and the delicious ingredients used here – fresh fruit, chocolate and marshmallow – mean that this recipe will be a popular choice with children and adults alike.

2 Mix together the butter, lemon juice and ground cinnamon and brush the mixture generously over the fruits.

3 For the fondue, place the chocolate, cream and marshmallows in a small pan and heat gently, without boiling, stirring continuously until the mixture has melted and is smooth.

INGREDIENTS

2 bananas
2 kiwi fruit
12 strawberries
15ml/1 tbsp melted butter
15ml/1 tbsp lemon juice
5ml/1 tsp ground cinnamon

FOR THE FONDUE
225g/8oz plain chocolate
120ml/4fl oz/½ cup single cream
8 marshmallows
2.5ml/½ tsp vanilla essence

SERVES 4

1 Peel the bananas and cut into thick chunks. Peel the kiwi fruit and quarter them. Thread the bananas, kiwi fruit and strawberries on to four wooden skewers. (Soak the skewers in water for 15 minutes beforehand to prevent them scorching on the barbecue.)

4 Cook the kebabs on a medium-hot barbecue for about 2–3 minutes, turning once, or until the fruit is golden. Stir the vanilla essence into the fondue. Empty the fondue into a small bowl and serve at once, with the fruit kebabs.

INDEX

• • •